A Lost Virtue &
The Search for Truth

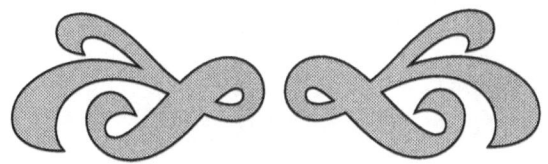

by

Lillian Carucio

authorHOUSE®

AuthorHouse™
1663 Liberty Drive, Suite 200
Bloomington, IN 47403
www.authorhouse.com
Phone: 1-800-839-8640

First published by AuthorHouse   1/9/2008

ISBN: 978-1-4343-5295-8 (sc)

Printed in the United States of America
Bloomington, Indiana

This book is printed on acid-free paper.

To my husband, family and friends,
whose encouragement and help throughout this endeavor
are so greatly appreciated.
And, especially to my mother whose love and inspiration
are always with me.

Contents

Introduction

Jesus, meek, and humble of heart,
make my heart like your heart.
(From the Act of Consecration to the Sacred Heart)

We are living in a world that has lost touch with God. Although many claim to believe in God, belief by itself is not enough. True belief is made up of faith, love, and obedience. If we do not ask God for the grace to love Him, to have faith in Him, and to do His will, it does not matter if we believe He exists. Satan believes God exists, but his belief will never get him to heaven. If we do not keep in touch with God by sincere daily prayer, we will lose our relationship with Him and will find ourselves on our own. God does not force Himself on anyone, even though He desires to be the most important person in your life and mine, to keep us from evil, and to bring us to everlasting life.

A recent survey, conducted by Gallop and analyzed by sociologists from Baylor University's Institute for Studies of Religion, revealed that nine out of ten Americans say they do believe in God. However, the survey showed that four different views of defining God exist. It is important to understand the different worldviews in order to understand what is happening. This book tries to explain how conservatism, liberalism, secularism, and humanism have changed the world and how we perceive God.

A Lost Virtue & The Search For Truth is written as a book of hope for the future, based on reflections of the past. We can learn from past disappointments, as well as from past achievements. If we face the failures honestly, we will find opportunities to learn, grow, and heal as individuals and as a nation. At the heart of this book is the belief that there *is* a right way and a wrong way and that they are based on an absolute *Truth*, revealed to us by our Creator. A search for this truth is necessary if we are to find our way through this life.

My hope is to help discern the truth, with logic and faith, from the misunderstandings, misinformation, and lies that are so prevalent in our society today. We have been led to believe many things that sound good, but have been proven to be unreliable. From the time of the French Revolution, through the Enlightenment, to the present time, there has been a trend to devalue tradition and the wisdom of the past. Many have begun to accept the idea that the beliefs of the past could be done away with, and a new and better world can be achieved.

It is always wise to look at what has gone on in the past before we venture into the future. It is foolish to think that we know everything. If we do not look to God, and to our forefathers before us, we are left to make our decisions on insufficient grounds. We can tell ourselves anything we want to hear. There is a succession of steps that have brought us to this modern worldview, and it is very interesting to note that those who had the greatest influence on our modern-day thinking were either atheists or men and women who did not trust God enough, and decided that they were more knowledgeable and able to improve world conditions without His help. Among some of these educators and philosophers are John Dewey, Sigmund Freud, Karl Marx, and Friedrich Nietzsche. They had no interest in saving souls, in eternal life, or in serving God. However, their atheistic influence has changed the world into one with a new worldview of morals.

One fact that has helped me to understand what has happened over the past few years is that most of those who have had such great influence in changing the worldview from a God-centered world to a man-centered world are all men and women who have little or no use for God. They were, and are, people who either think they do not need God or who think God has done a very poor job of ruling the universe. They are also people who do not accept the concept of sin and the consequences that are the result of sin.

There are several questions that can be asked: (1) Why were people happier and more content with their lot in life before the 1960's than they are today? (2) Why were people more civil to each other before the 1960's that they are today? And, (3) Why were honesty and integrity more important qualities before the 1960's than they are today? Those who want to blame America for every evil and those who hate the Christian worldview will tell us of slavery, discrimination, poverty, sexual and physical abuse, exploitation of some human beings by other human beings, and all the other ills that were part of the past. Slavery in America has been eliminated because of Christianity. We are working very hard to eliminate discrimination. Exploitation of human beings is not allowed in America. Poverty and abuse are still with us, even though much money has been spent to cure the problem of poverty. Political correctness has been tried, in the place of God, to eliminate sexual and physical abuse, but the problems still remain. Only a change of heart in each human being can make this a better world. It is God, not Government, who can change the human heart.

Something has gone wrong in America, and it is in our best interest to find out what has happened and what has to be done to really solve the problems that face us. What has happened to the American spirit? That spirit that is given by God to those who trust Him. It is the spirit that tells us the best we can do with our lives is to love God, country, family, and neighbor. America has always been a country of doers, with few complainers. This is what has made America a great nation. Today, all I seem to hear are complainers who do not have all the facts or who have no solutions to the problems. Complaining has never achieved anything worthwhile. It just drags everyone down. If we know that our government is corrupt, we, the people, have the power to change it. We do not have to complain and do nothing. We have to know for a fact who is corrupt and who is being falsely accused. Nothing can really be accomplished if we do not know the truth. When we can prove that someone is guilty of a crime, or is not qualified for the job he or she is doing, that is the time to remove him or her from the job. False witness is a sin, and I'm afraid there is too much of that going on today. There are certain things we know to be true. When the laws of God are followed, we see positive results. When we disobey the laws of God, we see negative results. This should be where we begin our investigation into what is true and what is false, what will work and what will fail, and why.

One program after another has been implemented to alleviate poverty and abuse, but the problems are still with us. We have created a welfare state with a dependency population. Women actually suffer more today from divorce and economic instability than they did in the past. Family cohesion has suffered terribly. We are seeing more family disorder and unhappy children than ever before. The problems of poverty cannot be solved by creating a dependency population. Much money has been spent on programs that do not work. Education is the best way to help those who are living in poverty. In many cases, we have parents who are not ready to be parents. We need good parents, good teachers, a good educational system, and a God-centered society. Bad parents, bad teachers, a bad educational system and a man-centered society only perpetuate the problem. It is up to the American people to choose whether they want to live with God in their lives, or if they want to live without Him.

There is no doubt that Christians have not done their job. We have been quiet while we let the secular humanists spread their ideas and beliefs, which conflict with the teachings of Jesus Christ. The war is on. Can we live with both Christianity and secular humanism? We are living with both now, but one has to prevail. One side has to win. As our world is falling apart, we have to decide if we want to believe God or to believe the humanists. They are on opposite sides of each other, so we cannot choose both.

We all know our public school system has been in serious trouble for some time. Learning has been replaced by indoctrination. The teaching principles that worked since the inception of our American school system have been replaced with political correctness, sensitivity training, situational ethics, relativism, conflict resolution, and experimentation.. Our educational system has been taken over by secular humanists and Marxists, who have succeeded in removing God from our public schools, and are in the process of trying to remove God from every aspect of our public lives.

The influence of John Dewey, an avowed atheist/humanist, has been a leading factor in abandoning authoritarian methods of teaching, and implementing a method of learning through experimentation and practical integration. Today, Dewey's instrumentalism and Karl Marx's socialistic ideas have taken over our public educational system. It is no surprise to anyone that some of our once great universities have become bastions of liberalism. It is also a fact that most of these university professors are secular humanists, who tend to believe that socialism/Marxism must replace capitalism. They do not seem to take into consideration the fact that capitalism, socialism, or democracy will self-destruct without morality. Capitalism stresses competition, profit, and private ownership of property, and works well when greed and corruption are not involved. Socialism calls for cooperation, social service, and government ownership of property, but has been unsuccessful because of much corruption, and also because of human nature and the many different types of people. There are givers and there are takers, self-centered people and selfless people. Some are problem-solvers, others are complainers who would rather have someone else solve their problems. Some people put much effort into their work, and some do not. Those who are truly in need must be helped, but we do not need socialism to do that. That is what Christianity does. Socialism claims that all people must be treated equally and fairly, but is it fair for those who work hard to carry the load for those who do not want to work?

It is interesting to study the ideas of men like John Dewey, Karl Marx, Sigmund Freud, Bertrand Russell, and Friedrich Nietzsche, and to compare their ideas and teachings with those of men like St. Augustine, C. S. Lewis, Fulton Sheen, Billy Graham, and Rabbi Harold Kushner. The atheistic humanists have little or no hope for humanity. They had a desire to improve the human condition, but their ideas have failed. The men of God have seen God through their sufferings, their pain, and their trials and errors, and have been successful. They know that it is through God's grace that they survive to see a hopeful future. They know that man is sinful and in need of redemption. The humanist believes man is basically good and is his own god, and there is no need for redemption because there is no sin. He mistakes freedom to choose God or to reject Him for license to deviate from the rule.

I am beginning to see something that is giving me hopeful optimism that the young people of this generation, and future generations, will begin to seek the true God of the Bible. I do see a glimmer of hope in many young men and women, those who are not seen in the mainstream media, who are turning to God for guidance in their lives. Many of these young people are not satisfied with our popular culture. They believe there is something bigger than themselves and a greater meaning to life. They are seeking truth; they are seeking God. Life cannot be beautiful when there is so much hatred and deceit going on.

I began this project trying to be optimistic, but there were many times I felt despair for God, for my religion, and for my country. My hope is, as I knew it had to be, in our young people. Many of the baby-boomers were raised by parents who had turned away from the strict, conservative religions they had been raised in. They began to believe that perhaps life didn't have to be so hard, that there must be some way to alleviate suffering, and that a good and loving God would not expect so much goodness from mere human beings.

There were many reasons for creating a god that suited their wants, their needs, and desires. This god was a god of "love" with no strings attached. Permissiveness and tolerance became the rule. There was no right or wrong. There were situational ethics. The door had been opened for moral decay. This new religion might be understandable if one believes there is no such thing as sin, that the moral teachings of the past were just that - - - past. And that we have now entered a more enlightened world. It is not understandable if one believes the truth that God has given us. A rebellion against all authority, including God, became evident in the sixties, and in many ways continues today. My fear was never that God would lose the war. My fear is that if America loses God, America will lose the war.

This is not a book about conservatism or liberalism. It is a book about Christianity and about seeking the truth. One may say Christianity is not conservative or liberal, or one may say Christianity is both conservative and liberal. There is truth to both of those statements. Are people really looking for the truth, or are we becoming more cynical and nasty? The problem, as I see it, is a lack of truth on all sides. Where does all the false information come from? Why are we all fighting with one another, rather than working together as God intended?

For over two hundred years, Americans have had no problem living in a Judeo-Christian nation, which allowed people of different religions to practice whatever religion they wished to practice. Christianity does not force anyone to do anything, but all Christians are asked by Jesus Christ to spread His gospel to all the world because it is the truth. America has been a shining beacon to the world. God has blessed His people. We must continue to seek God's wisdom and ask Him to bless America.

Humility, The Lost Virtue

When pride comes, then comes disgrace, but with
humility comes wisdom
Proverbs 11:2

There is no doubt something is terribly wrong in this world. We all want to blame someone, preferably someone else. Liberals blame conservatives. Conservatives blame liberals. Democrats blame Republicans. Republicans blame Democrats. Religious people blame secularists. Secularists blame religious people. We are in the middle of the greatest fight in history. The next few years will determine the future course of the world. We are in a war, and this war is for the minds and hearts of individuals.

There are many questions to be answered. We are inundated with lies, half truths, and spin. We must examine each question with an open mind and a request (a sincere prayer) to God to help us discern the truth from the lies. This is a war between Christianity and atheism. There is no doubt that God will win this war. The question is whose side America will be on. Where can we get some answers? This is where humility plays a part. There is no way to please God if we do not humble ourselves and seek His guidance, and God will not answer us if we think we know more than He does.

In his book, *Mere Christianity*, C. S. Lewis tells us:

> *In God you come up against something which is in every respect immeasurably superior to yourself. Unless you know God as that - - and, therefore, know yourself as nothing in comparison - - you do not know God as that - - and, therefore, know yourself as nothing in comparison - - you do not know God at all. As long as you are proud you cannot know God. A proud man is always looking down on things and people: and, of course, as long as you are looking down, you cannot see something that is above you. That raises a terrible question. How is it that people who are quite obviously eaten up with Pride can say they believe in God and appear to themselves very religious? I am afraid it means they are worshipping an imaginary God.*
>
> ---- *C. S. Lewis,*
> *Mere Christianity 124*

It all begins with humility. Of all the virtues, humility is first, because without it, we will find the other virtues very difficult to practice. Virtues do not seem to have much value in our modern society, and humility seems to be a quality of the past. But without humility, one cannot be true to oneself or to anyone else. A humble person knows he or she has to look to God for help because God has the answers. Whether we realize it or not, every one of us is looking for moral character in the people in our lives and in our public officials, but what about ourselves? To be humble is to be willing and able to acknowledge our weaknesses and defects, our strengths and special gifts, without conceit. To be humble is to know who you are and to be grateful to God for everything He has given you. To be humble before God is to acknowledge His holiness and superiority.

To be humble does not make one a weak person. When a person is humble before God, he receives the grace and strength that can only come from God. He realizes that he is dependent on God as well as himself. Humility is the opposite of pride and arrogance.

Also, humility is the good part of self-esteem. If one knows who he is in the eyes of God, he does not have to be overly concerned about what others say or think about him. People come in all varieties, and there will always be some who will not like us.

Jesus was the strongest and most powerful person who has ever lived in this world, yet He was meek and humble. He was not arrogant, prideful, or self-centered. He knew that He was here for a purpose, and He lived every day of His life true to that purpose. We are also here for a purpose. God has a purpose for your life. It is up to you whether you choose God's plan for your life or whether you choose to live your life without Him. He has given you free will, and He will not force Himself where He is not wanted.

In the place of humility today, our young people are getting the message that to be self-serving and aggressive is the way to go. Too many parents do not know how, or refuse, to discipline their children, thus giving young people the idea that the world has been made for them. God did not create the world for you (or for me). He created the earth for Himself. He is willing to share it with us. He is not willing to let us take it over. The message is also being sent that honesty does not always get you where you think you want to go. If we are not good role models, what will the consequences be? Our children must be taught to respect themselves and others. We must help them to understand that the world does not revolve around them and there are some things that are more important than having fun and obtaining a lot of material things. We have to teach them to be grateful for what has been given to them. We all have a responsibility for the future of our country, and the future of our country depends on our children. We are all looking for the secret to happiness. Some have begun to think that humanism is the answer.

The word *humanism"* has many meanings. The two types of Humanism I am concerned with are Christian Humanism and Secular Humanism. Christian Humanism is defined as a *philosophy"* advocating the self-fulfillment of man within the framework of Christian principles.

(*Webster's Third New International Dictionary*). Secular Humanism is defined as outgrowth of 18th century enlightenment and 19th century free-thought.. (*What Is A Humanist?, Frederick Edwards*) Secularism is defined as a system of doctrines and practices that rejects any form of religious faith and worship. Belonging to the world and worldly things as distinguished from the church and religious affairs. (*Webster's New World Dictionary*).

> *The most critical irony in dealing with Modern Humanism is the inability of its advocates to agree on whether or not this worldview is religious. Those who see it as a philosophy are the Secularist Humanists while those who see it as a religion are the Religious Humanists.*
>
> (*What Is A Humanist?*,
> *Frederick Edwards*).

Happiness will never come from just getting things you want. That is temporary pleasure. True happiness comes from serving God and your fellow man.. When we are concerned about one another, we find a fulfillment that does not come from obtaining material things. Because we have become such a materialistic society, many no longer take God seriously. A physical thing is something we can feel and touch, but God is spirit. We must find God through faith.

How did we lose God? God is not lost. He is where He has always been and where He always will be. We are the lost sheep. We have turned away from God towards humanism. It is not God who has neglected us. He has given us our instructions for living. The Bible is not made up of a lot of words written by some men who wanted to make the lives of human beings miserable. Rather, the Bible has been given to us by God so that we may know the meaning and purpose of life. The Bible is the word of God, written by men who were inspired by the Holy Spirit. There is not a book that is more inspiring or instructive than the Bible.

Many Christian clerics, the very people we depend on for religious truth, have let us down by preaching a watered-down version of Christianity. It seems as if they have not only lost their humility, but their faith as well. I have been very interested in liberal theology and liberation theology. I have been asking myself why some Christian clerics were turning against the teachings of their churches and denominations. What were they disagreeing with? My answer came in *Exodus*, a very interesting and informative book written by Dave Shiflett. He writes, "*The clerics are doing missionary work, though not of the sort one would imagine. They have considered God's ways, as revealed in their faith's Scriptures and traditions, and found them wanting. (Exodus 24)*. It may be that the liberal clerics truly feel that they have a better understanding of God's will, or as David Shiflett writes, "*They have a higher agenda to advance, one that promises to improve upon a failed God." (Exodus 24)*.

What has happened to the humility and faith in the spiritual lives of these clerics? Have they turned their backs on the God of the Bible and created an image of a god who appeals to their agendas? In many cases, their agendas may be sinful, but they no longer believe in a judgmental God. They believe in a God who loves and forgives, with no questions asked. They call themselves Christians, but a Christian is a follower of Christ in all things.

There is no middle ground with God. We have only two choices. We can choose God or we can choose ourselves. When we choose to live our lives outside of God's will, we are putting ourselves in the hands of Satan. Life is not a vacuum. We are constantly being influenced by either the Holy Spirit or Satan. That may be hard to accept in our modern society, but either God exists or He does not. If God exists, it is in our best interest to believe Him and try to be an obedient child of God. If God does not exist, then for many of us, this life makes no sense. It would mean there is no truth in the Bible and Jesus was not who He said He was, the Son of God, the second member of the Trinity. You can either believe Jesus or call Him a liar.

I have to admit that liberal Christianity sounds very appealing. Every message seems positive at first glance. Praise for God and one another, love, joy, and hope for everyone is preached. Not only is the message appealing, it also sounds very compassionate. The "compassionate" message is disingenuous because it does not include the whole truth. At Unity Church in Chelsea, New York, Paul Geneglia opened his sermon by saying, *"Welcome to Unity of New York! This is one church where you will not be told that you are a miserable sinner." (A New Christianity for a New World, John Shelby Spong, Newsletter)*. We may not all be *miserable* sinners, but we are all sinners and in need of God.

There is no mention of sin, repentance, or the importance of the sacraments, because there are no sinners. No matter what we do, it is acceptable. Yet, we know sin exists and sin is not acceptable to God. We know there are consequences for our actions, and pain and suffering are the consequences of sin. In one way or another, we have all sinned against God, whether we admit it or not. It is the liberal theologians who no longer seem to recognize the fact that sin and evil exist, and that everyone has a need to recognize his or her sin, to ask God for forgiveness, and to repent.

In my study of European history, I began to see how God was slowly being pushed out of a god-centered society as a secular humanistic society began to emerge. Although a humanist movement had been in progress since the seventeenth century, it was not effective. In fact, atheists and agnostics were considered out of the mainstream.

During the eighteenth century, a period called the Enlightenment, when scientific and technological information was increasing, philosophers began to openly criticize the authority of the church. There were debates regarding faith against reason. Many philosophers began to reject faith in favor of reason alone. Theologians and philosophers, who valued the human mind and reason above all, began to believe that people should be active and engaged in this life, and not worry or plan for either damnation or paradise in the next.

The Renaissance period had produced advancements in all areas of human potential. The mind of man was expanded, the New World was discovered, and a scientific revolution was beginning. The invention of the printing press had a profound impact on the spread of knowledge all over the world. It was the beginning of "how great we are," rather than "how great Thou art."

The other evening, I was watching a World War II movie, and I was struck by what we believed at that time and what is happening today. As I watched the movie, I began to realize that evil is still with us, even though we thought the end of the war had eliminated evil for all time. No sooner was World War II over than we had to deal with the Korean War, the Vietnam War, and the Cold War, all against communism. We had eliminated one kind of war and one kind of enemy only to be faced, after sixty years, with a new kind of war and a new kind of enemy, an enemy we never could have imagined.

We were jubilant in 1945 when the war ended. We thought we had fought and won our last war. Of course, this is also what we believed after World War I. We were ready to build a world of peace and prosperity. For a short time, the late 40s and the 50s were a time of hope and happiness. Why didn't the world of the 50s continue?

Until the 1960s, the world was pretty much centered around God. Most Americans were raised to believe God was the creator of the universe, and we were taught to be obedient and grateful to Him. We acknowledged a moral standard of right and wrong. We knew some things were good and some things were evil. We knew that God knows every thought and deed. It is a lot easier to be good when we know that someone is watching. It is much more desirable to our human nature to talk ourselves into believing that we have a right to privacy and no one else knows what we are thinking or doing, but that is wishful thinking. We believed in a cause bigger than ourselves. In the 1960s, our beliefs began to change. We began to lose our faith in the God of the Bible, and we are beginning to see the results of that kind of thinking.

A rebellion in America was beginning in the 1960s. Although the Vietnam War turned out to be a disaster, the original intent was to stop communism from expanding all over the world. This gave some an excuse, including theologians and clerics, who had been drawn to liberal thinking, to change the rules. We no longer had to fear God, because *sin* was a word from the past. There was no right or wrong. Everything was relative. We were to love everyone, except those Christians who were trying to impose their beliefs and morals on the rest of us. It was the beginning of political correctness.

For the past forty years, we have been trying to replace the true teachings of Jesus Christ with a counterfeit political correctness. We cannot replace God, and it is because of pride in the place of humility that we think it may be possible.

Character / Obedience / Conscience

And we rejoice in the hope of the glory of God. Not only
so, but we also rejoice in our sufferings, because we know
that suffering produces perseverance; perseverance,
character, and character, hope.
Romans 5:1-4

Humility is not the only virtue that is in short supply today. Men and women of strong and moral character seem to be in the minority. Parents have failed, teachers have failed, and society all have failed in their obligation to instill and reinforce necessary values (virtues), such as honesty, respect, responsibility, courtesy, self-discipline, obedience, prudence, and the value of chastity in our young people, those virtues that are necessay for a meaningful and successful God-given life. Also lacking is the courage to stand against those who are determined to remove God from our public schools. The importance of diligence and excellence has been de-emphasized and mediocrity in academics has become acceptable. The breakup of families, sacrilegious films, television programs, athletes and public officials with little integrity or honesty make very poor role models for those who depend on us for guidance.

As our children are growing into young adults, we must give them positive examples of honesty and a reason to strive for excellence. Good character is not what we are instilling in our children today. Many of them do not even believe it is wrong to lie, to cheat, or to steal to get what they want. Discipline builds character. Permissiveness creates weakness.

Without a good moral character, a person will make a mess of his or her life. It is God's will that we allow Him to help us in building our character. God cares about each person's integrity, conscience, heart, and soul, and it is the Holy Spirit who helps us to become Christ-like, to build a strong and moral character.

When our public school educators find it necessary to ban God from the classroom and replace truth with their ideas of tolerance, justice, equality, political correctness, sensitivity training, self-esteem, and sex education, we are going down a path that will lead to destruction. These educators have no right to replace God's words and the truths that have been handed down from generation to generation, but that is exactly what they have done, and are still doing. If we do not wake up from our complacency, we will leave a world to our children that will bring them nothing but despair. There was a time when we knew that children must be taught obedience, respect, honesty, the ability to read, to spell correctly, to become proficient in mathematics, and the true history of this great country. There has been an erosion of standards, and excellence has been replaced by mediocrity. A value-neutral cultural sensitivity has replaced the teaching of good behavior and responsible citizenship. If these man-made ideas had produced some positive results, I would have nothing to write about on this subject, but the secular and liberal policies of the past forty years have been disastrous. Young people were once taught that there is a greater good and a higher power. Now they are being taught to believe in themselves alone. We have been leading our children astray, and the evidence is before our very eyes.

How foolish is it to teach our children that freedom is free when the exact opposite is true? We are a free people because someone before us fought and died for our freedom, and we have been silent long enough. The war against God is on, and if we do nothing, we will be in great danger of losing everything our heroes have fought for, both in the past and those heroes of today who are fighting to protect us and our American way of life.

We are now living in a world of confusion, disobedience, and disregard for the moral and social standards God has given us. Do we really care about God and the moral truths He has given us? How true are we to God? How we see God determines the way we respond to Him. What we believe about God is the basis of our belief system. I believe that if we are to be honest with ourselves, we cannot believe God exists and not believe what He has revealed. Either God exists or He does not. There are many reasons one may choose to not believe the truth of the Bible. The truth is sometimes painful, but to choose to believe untruthfulness does not change the truth.

Life is difficult. We ask why life must be so difficult, and God tells us that pain and suffering are part of the human condition because of sin. We find it difficult to believe that the laws of God are the best way to live our lives, because our human nature does not agree. God's ways are not easy, and we would always rather find the easy way rather than the hard way, but the easy way does not build character. It is through perseverance and dependence on God through our pain and suffering that we grow in character and spiritual maturity.

Love or Lust

*Love is patient, love is kind. It does not envy, it
does not boast. It is not proud. It is not rude,
it is not self-seeking, it is not easily angered,
it keeps no record of wrongs. Love does not
delight in evil, but rejoices with the truth.*
1 Corinthians 13:4-6

It is by giving that we receive. Love is a two-way street. God loves us with an unconditional love, but He asks for our willing love and obedience so that we will not condemn ourselves to hell. The description St. Paul gives us of love is very beautiful. He is speaking of the unconditional love, which is the true love of God, and the only love that will bring us true happiness. The world we live in today knows little of this kind of love. Although each one of us may be looking for this type of love in another person, many of us are not willing to let God work out this kind of love in our own lives.

This true love is the essence of our being because it is God. Without love, we are lost souls. There is a great misconception of the real meaning of love in our modern society. There is no doubt that everyone believes that love is a very important emotion, but the idea of love has been greatly distorted. St. Paul is not talking about the syrupy counterfeit of love that exists today. Nor is he speaking of selfish love or dominating love.

We are living in a counterfeit world, a man-centered world rather than a God-centered world. As this world is slowly being turned away from God, we are seeing a loss of real love, humility, and moral character. When we lived in a God-centered world, we were more inclined to be obedient to the laws of God. Some tried to live by the laws of God out of love, and some out of a fear of going to hell. Whatever the reason, we all knew what was right and what was wrong. Relativity was not a part of the equation. Today we have little or no respect or concern for God or His laws. Proverbs 9:10 tells us, *"The fear of the Lord is the beginning of wisdom, and knowledge of the Holy One is understanding."* God asks us to be obedient out of love for Him rather than fear of Him. But the fear of God is the beginning of wisdom, and without wisdom, it is very difficult to make proper decisions.

We crave whatever is pleasing to our senses, whether it is good for us or not. Our human nature is not necessarily our best friend. If left alone, our human nature will lead us away from God instead of towards Him. Love comes from God; lust comes from Satan. We must be sure we are traveling in the right direction. Love is a very beautiful thing; lust is the opposite. Love requires self-sacrifice on our part, but it brings great reward. Lust requires nothing from us but momentary pleasure, but it brings nothing but disappointment, pain, and suffering. *"Put to death, therefore, whatever belongs to your earthly nature; sexual immorality, impurity, lust, evil desires, and greed, which is idolatry. Because of these, the wrath of God is coming."* (Colossians 3:5-6).

This world has become obsessed with sexual immorality, impurity, lust, evil desires, and greed, but very little real love. Many in our society seem to believe that sex is as important to life as breathing. Even though St. Paul tells us that all sex outside of marriage is sinful, very few people seem to be able to accept that message. Secular humanism has convinced most Americans that sex is free and everyone has a right to enjoy it in any way he or she wishes.

We are all looking for love, whether it is romantic love, family love, love of neighbor, or love of country. What we see is too much hatred and not enough love. We must also keep in mind that love is more than an emotion. We fool ourselves when we limit our love to good feelings only. Love is also, and more importantly in the eyes of God, a matter of the will. Jesus tells us to love our neighbor as ourselves (whether we like our neighbor or not). We are to wish him well. We do not have to like our neighbor, but we are to love him.

When we do not let God into our lives, we open the door to Satan. We tell ourselves we are good people who do some things we know are wrong, but we forget to tell ourselves that we are sinners and that our sins bring consequences. What we do not remember is that God is holy and that He cannot abide sin. If sin were not so abhorrent to God, there would have been no reason for Jesus to die on the cross for our sins.

We are bombarded by vulgarity and filth, and we are laughed at if we are offended. Christians are not to be offended; they must learn to be tolerant and non-judgmental of any immorality they know is offensive to God. More and more sinful behavior has become acceptable and considered normal. We must be humble before God, so that we can see our true selves and the truth of God.

Political correctness and the radical feminist movement have turned our world upside down. Many women feel they have to take over the roles of men in order to be equal. Although the feminist movement has lost much of its momentum, the damage has been done. Many young women continue to believe that they must assert themselves against the power of men. There is no way love can grow in this kind of gender war. God made men and women to complement one another and to love one another, not to be the same, and to hate one another.

Men and women are equal in the eyes of God. They are equal human beings with different roles. Some women are smarter than some men, and also some women. Some men are smarter than some women, and also some men. We cannot categorize individuals. Everyone is different and God has given each one of us some gift or talent, and we are asked to use that gift to the best of our abilities.

Sex is not a means of recreation. We must not mistake lust or infatuation for love. True love between a man and a woman leads to marriage. God tells us that sex outside of marriage is wrong, and it is harmful to our well-being, but our modern society laughs at God. Infatuation and lust are not love, and neither lasts very long. They are both very strong emotions, and they both bring heartbreak and sorrow, not to mention mental and physical illness. There is no fulfillment in lust or infatuation. If we want to live happy and meaningful lives, we have to learn the difference between love, lust, and infatuation. Lust is a self-fulfilling emotion; true love is selfless consideration of the loved one, infatuation can be defined as being carried away by an unreasoning passion or attraction and lacking sound judgment.

Sin and God

Therefore, just as sin entered the world through one man, and death through sin, and in this way death came to all men, because all sinned - - - for before the law was given, sin was in the world. But sin is not taken into account when there is no law.
Romans 5:12-13

Sin has been defined as the willful breaking of religious or moral law. Because of His holiness, God cannot accept sin. Whether we realize it or not, there has been an attempt to eliminate the idea that there is such a thing as sin, but it is impossible to believe in God and not believe that sin exists. Sin entered the world very shortly after God created man, and it has been with us ever since. We can neglect the word, but we cannot neglect or eliminate the fact that sin does exist, and that we are all guilty of sin because we have all broken a moral law at one time or another. Because some do not want to believe in moral law, or a creator who has given us moral law, the concept that all matters are relative has become acceptable. It is to our detriment that many of our clergy have also adopted this false belief. An offense against God's law does not become inoffensive just because we decide it is no longer offensive. Since sin is a willful act, I am not in a position to know how God will deal with those who unknowingly offend God because they have been taught Satan's lies instead of God's truth. However, ignorance of the law does not prevent the consequences.

Everyone's view of the world depends on his or her view of God. Those who believe the words of the God of the Bible see their world as a response to God. Those who do not believe the words of the God of the Bible see the world as a place where they must do what they think is best because they are on their own and need to respond to no one.

In order to believe that there is no sin, a person would have to believe that God does not exist. If one believes that there is no God, it becomes easy to believe that sin does not exist. For those who doubt the existence of God, and for those who believe that God does exist, but His moral laws do not apply to them, there are several questions that remain unanswered. We know we have intelligence and reason. Where did they come from? It is because of our God-given intelligence and reason that we, in our false pride, have convinced ourselves that we are in charge and that there is no need for God. It is through humility and faith that we can know God. When Jesus said, *"Blessed are the meek, for they will inherit the earth,"* He was telling us that only through humility would we be able to find Him. (Matthew 5:5).   Pride is the opposite of humility.   Pride tells us to worship ourselves.   Humility tells us we are to worship God.

We also know that when the moral laws of God are followed, we have a decent and respectable society, and when the moral laws are ignored, we have what we are seeing today. The argument that man's reason tells him that God's existence or the value of His laws cannot be substantiated is not convincing. We know there is a moral law, and we know that a moral law is necessary for a morally functional, civil, and courteous society.   In other words, reason tells us that a moral law is necessary, and must come from somewhere. *"For I, the Lord your God, am a jealous God, visiting the iniquity of the fathers on the children to the third and fourth generations of those who hate Me, but showing mercy to a thousand generations, of those who love Me and keep my Commandments."* (Exodus 20:4-6).

This life on earth is not easy; the further we move away from God, the more difficult our lives become. Is God punishing us for our disobedience? I see a world going out of control, and more unhappiness and discontent than I could ever have imagined, but I do not believe that this is God's punishment.   I am afraid that we will continue on this path of destruction if we do not bring God back into our lives. I do believe that He allows, but does not cause, some disasters to wake us up. The Bible teaches us that *"God is love."* We sometimes mistake God's love as non-judgmental and tolerant rather than unconditional. We want to believe that if God really loves us, He would want us to be happy; therefore, we should be able to do whatever we believe will make us happy.   In his book, *Is God To Blame?,* Gregory A. Boyd writes, "*Of course he could have created a world where we 'have' to do his will, but it would have been a creation devoid of love.*" The truth is that God does want us to be happy and He also knows we are not the best judge of what will make us happy. We are very often inclined to make some very bad choices. Because God has chosen to give us a free will, we often choose to reject His will. Is God angry with us? I tend to believe that He is more heartbroken than angry, but He certainly is not pleased, and He certainly knows what is going on.

Does God answer prayer? Yes, He does. However, there is a *BUT.* God is not our servant.   *But - - -* He asks that we be His. This is not a command; it is a request to love and serve the Lord, your God, and your fellow man. It is apparent that not many people pay very much attention, or even believe that there is any truth to this request. God also asks us to keep in touch. We cannot just send up prayers when we want a favor. Our praying must be persistent. We must talk to Him every day. When we pray, we should ask God to make our hearts like His heart. That is a prayer He always answers and He gives His blessings to those who desire to do His will. He blesses those who seek His grace in all things. Those who ask Him to keep us from evil,. "*Therefore, O house of Israel, I will judge you, each one according to his ways, declares the*

Sovereign Lord. Repent! Turn away from all your offenses; then sin will not be your downfall. (Ezekiel 18:30).   There is no doubt that if we all did love and serve God and our fellow man, this world would be a better world.

Another word that seems to have disappeared from the English language is *duty.* When Americans were aware of the fact that they had duties to God and country, we had a much happier and more civilized society. Neglecting one's duty may not necessarily be a sin, but it does help to diminish one's character.   Character is built on losing oneself to God, and doing one's best for the welfare of others.   It is not only people in the military who have duties to God and country; we all have such duties.   Our duties may not all be the same, but we all have them. We have duties to God, to our country, and to our families. A husband and father has a duty to take care of and provide for his family; a wife and mother has a duty to help her husband and to nurture their children. Children have a duty to obey their parents and their teachers, and to respect adults.   It is the knowledge that there is something bigger than we are, that this life is a testing ground and that we are destined for an eternal life of happiness, that gives life meaning. This message is the only message that gives life meaning, because it is the only true message. This life on earth is not easy, and that is because we would rather choose a sinful life than a holy life. If God had not given us free will, we would have been obedient, loyal, and holy, with no desire to sin. However, God has given us free will with which to either choose Him or reject Him.

In trying to explain the existence of evil in the world, C. S. Lewis tells us that, although intelligence and free will are good in themselves, the capacity to do evil must follow.   In his book *Mere Christianity,* C. S. Lewis writes:

> *"God created things which had a free will. That means creatures which can go either wrong or right. Some people think that they can imagine a creature which was free but*

had no possibility of going wrong.   I cannot.   If a thing is free to be good it is also free to be bad.   And free will is what has made evil possible.   Why then, did God give them free will?   Because free will, though it makes evil possible, is the only thing that makes possible any love or goodness or joy worth having.

---- C. S. Lewis,
Mere Christianity 47-48

He also explains, *"But pleasure, money, power, and safety are all, as far as they go, good things.   The badness consists in pursuing them by the wrong method, or in the wrong way, or too much.   Goodness is, so to speak, itself; badness is only spoiled goodness.   And there must be something good first before it can be spoiled."* (Mere Christianity 44).

There are many things we cannot understand.   But, it is not as important to understand as to trust in Jesus Christ. He came to us; He will come again; and now, He asks us to come to Him, to trust Him, and to love Him as He loves us.

Mary or Eve

Behold the handmaid of the Lord,
be it done according to thy word.
Luke 1:38

God has given us a perfect role model in Mary, the mother of Jesus. We can look to her to see the qualities God admires. She was faithful, loving, humble, and obedient. These traits are not to be mistaken with weakness. There was no weakness in Mary. She had the strength and grace that God gives those who trust in Him. Imagine her strength and grace as she had to watch her son die on the cross.

Mary had strength and grace, but she was also powerful, because she had great influence with Jesus. It was in answer to Mary's request that Jesus performed His first miracle, even though He said His hour had not yet come: *"And on the third day a marriage took place at Cana of Galilee, and the mother of Jesus was there. Now Jesus too was invited to the marriage, and also His disciples. And the wine having run short, the mother of Jesus said to Him, 'They have no wine.' And Jesus said to her, 'What woudst thou have me do, woman? My hour has not yet come.' His mother said to the attendants, 'Do whatever He tells you.'"* (John 2: 1-5)..

Mary understood that God has a plan for each life. It is up to each one of us whether we accept His plan or insist on our own. She was submissive to God, in that she was humble and willing to be obedient to His will. Her submission was voluntary. God did not give her an order, nor was she a slave. To submit to God, because one understands the purpose of submission and feels it is the right thing to do, brings a peace and fulfillment that is not found without God in making decisions. To submit to God, or to anyone else, out of fear or weakness, is not the submissiveness that is asked for by God.

Another type of role model is Eve. Eve was not satisfied with what God had given her. She wanted more, and she got what she asked for. She lost her innocence because she disobeyed God. The story has not changed. We are still tempted today, as Eve was. We would all like to have more of the good things, and less boredom and suffering. We can follow Mary, the mother of Jesus, or Eve, the mother of the human race. Because of her humility and obedience to God, Mary has been revered by all. Eve, by her pride and disobedience to God, has brought pain and suffering to all.

Radical feminism is the exact opposite of the ideals Mary believed in. We can say that times have changed and women have come a long way, but human nature is the same today as it was in the time of Jesus. We tend to be self-centered, prideful, hateful, arrogant, and to want things our own way, rather than being obedient and faithful to God. It is humility that tells us to re-evaluate the situation before we storm ahead with our emotions, rather than our intellect. It takes time and prayer to make a wise decision.

The feminist movement has brought unnecessary pain and suffering to both women and men. Girls are being told to be more like boys, and men and boys are being feminized. This is not God's plan; this is a manmade plan that will never work. Why and how did we get to a place where we want to believe that there is no difference between men and women? The loss of humility and an overabundance of false pride and self-importance has played a large part in this change in society. Boredom and a desire for power on the part of some women also enter into the picture. But, the real reason is a rebellion against God's will, His plan, for men and women. In God's plan, women and men are equal, but different. They each have their roles to play. Men and women must complement one another. That is the way God planned it. As Dr. Laura Schlessinger says in her book *Woman Power*, *"We women have to take responsibility for how we raise our sons as well as how we present 'woman-hood' to the men in our lives. When, for example, 'nice girls didn't,' boys were clear that there were lofty values and ideals to aim high for. When men were expected to support their families, they worked hard to qualify for the hand of a good woman." (Woman Power 29).* It was a time when values were high, sex was not free, and both boys and men knew there were boundaries. Love was about marriage and commitment, not just sex, and without marriage and commitment there was no sex.

Dr. Schlessinger also writes: *"The true nature of a woman is to nurture; that should not be denied. When women are burdened by the pain, hopelessness, and helplessness of a failed marriage and family . . . that is the ultimate burden. What women accept or reject gives a clear message to men about the boundaries of their behavior if they wish to enjoy that affection and awe from their women. I am reaffirming the power of women to transform men, their families, and their lives. That power is not a burden. . . . it is a blessing." (Women Power 31).*

We have come to believe that there is inequality between men and women. There are good reasons for this seeming inequality. Discrimination of any kind is wrong and should be rectified. All persons should be paid the same wage for doing the same job. Equal pay for equal work is not disputed. However, while all men must work to support themselves and their families, all women are not required to support their families monetarily. Most women desire to be wives and mothers. Some do not. Some women would like to be housewives who can stay home to raise their children. Some would like to be wives and mothers who may have a part-time job. Some would like to have a full-time career. There is nothing wrong with any of these choices. The problem is that women were convinced by the feminists that they could have it all. We cannot have it all. Something has to give. There is also the very serious problem of women who are in a position where they must work and try to raise their children at the same time because of wrong choices or because of circumstances beyond their control. There are many problems and many choices to be made. The proposed purpose of the feminist movement was to make life better for women; it has not accomplished its proposed purpose.

If power is what a woman is looking for, she has been given that by God. She has the God-given ability to nurture and transform those in her life whom she loves. Some women are less than pleased, if not downright angry, with God's plan for the human race to survive. There is the mistaken belief by some women today that men see them only as sex objects. There may be more truth to this today than ever before, because some women have let themselves become nothing more than sex objects. However, real men do not fall in love with sex objects. They fall in love with real women of character and high moral values.

It is when a man or a woman demands more power than is rightfully his or hers that the problems begin. A person who is humble before God is grateful for whatever God has given her or him, and does not have a desire to rebel or to change the rules in order to get what she or he thinks is better.

I would encourage every person who is interested in finding the truth regarding his or her existence on this earth to study Christianity with an open mind.   Christianity is the only religion that answers the questions regarding life, death, and eternal life.   It is amazing to me that so few people sincerely seek the truth.   Is it because we are too busy, is it because we would rather believe whatever makes us feel good, or is it because we believe science has all the answers?

Christanity

I am the way and the truth and the life. No one comes
to the Father except through me. If you really knew
me you would know my Father as well. From now
on, you do know Him and have seen Him.
John 14:6

The claim has been made that Christianity is authoritative and repressive. Christians do claim that there is a supreme authority and Christianity does ask that we restrain ourselves from committing sin. The supreme authority is God. Christianity is a religion that preaches the teachings received from Jesus Christ and His apostles. Christians believe that Jesus Christ, the Son of God, willingly gave His life so that our sins could be forgiven. If Christianity is repressive, it is because a holy God cannot abide sin, and because the consequences of sin will produce death, whether it is death of the soul or the body.

Christians are accused of trying to force their religion on everyone else. That is a lie. American Christians are trying to hold on to the beliefs that have been theirs since the beginning of this great country. It is the secularists who are trying to force their godless religion on an unsuspecting society. Jesus did not force anyone to believe Him, and neither do His followers. Because Christians know that Jesus died for their sins, and for the sins of all mankind, they do not want to keep the good news to themselves. They want to share it with mankind, as Jesus asked them to do: *"Go into all the world and preach the good news to all creation".* (Mark 16:15).

Are God's laws restrictive and repressive? To our human nature, they surely seem to be. When we choose to act against God's moral laws, we sin against God. Is it possible to live a sinless life without the help of God? I know that I cannot, and I don't know anyone who has been able to. The Bible tells us there is not one who leads a sinless life. We are all sinners in one way or another, and the consequences of sin is death. It is because we are all sinners that God, in His mercy, sent His Son, Jesus Christ, to give us another chance. Our human nature will lead us to evil, but with the grace of God, we can overcome evil. Jesus said, *"I am the vine, you are the branches. If a man remains in me and I in him, he will bear much fruit, apart from me, you can do nothing.* (John 15:5).

The attack on Christianity is something to be worried about. It is getting stronger because too many Christians cannot see what is happening. Why is Christianity the only religion that must be kept out of the public arena? There is a good reason for this. Christianity is God calling you and me to Himself. Without the interference from Satan in the form of secularism, many would hear Him and answer His call. It is very clear that the secularist/atheist movement does not want this to happen. As far as they are concerned, Christian morals will take away the immoral freedoms they desire to expand.

> *"If the world hates you, keep in mind that it hated me first. They will treat you this way beause of my name, for they do not know the One who sent me. If I had not come and spoken to them, they would not be guilty of sin. Now, however, they have no excuse for their sin. He who hates me, hates my Father as well".*
>
> (John 15-21).

The secularist, atheist, or liberal Christian limits his or her idea of morality to helping people they deem to be helpless, to being non-judgmental, and to being tolerant, even though their kindness seems to apply only to people who agree with them. Secularism and liberalism are not compatible with Christianity. The morality of Jesus encompasses so much more. A Christian knows Jesus is God, the second person of the Trinity, who gave His life for sinning mankind, who has sent the Holy Spirit to lead His followers through this life, and who is waiting for us to share eternity with Him in heaven. A Christian believes all the teachings of the Bible because they are the word of God: *"I can do everything through Him who gives me strength."* (Phil. 4:13)

America, as a Judeo-Christian nation, allows freedom of religion for everyone. Jesus said, *"Give to Caesar what is Caesar's, and to God what is God's." (Matt. 22:21)*. By saying "the things that belong to Caesar," Jesus was saying that God entrusts government authorities to maintain civil order, to punish wrongdoers, to protect their citizens, and to collect taxes to administer these functions. However, only God deserves our worship. All human government is subject to His higher authority and purpose to administer these functions.

Christianity teaches us that God is love and there can be true, lifelong, loving relationships. However, nothing worthwhile in this life is easy. It takes a lot of hard work, commitment, unselfishness, and sacrifice to find the kind of love that brings real happiness. Of most importance in God's plan for the human race is marriage. This union between a man and woman was instituted by God to ensure the propagation of the human race... From marriage, families are born. That is the plan. There is nothing more important than the proper raising of children, for their education, and for their spiritual growth. I know there are no perfect parents, and there never have been, but I do not know of a time in history when parents, teachers, society, and the media have caused so much damage to or have been so neglectful of the generation that followed them.

The *"Me"* generation had little opportunity to learn the true teachings of Jesus, because they were raised during the great rebellion. They were told that whatever seemed true to them was acceptable. But, there is only one truth, one perfect standard, and that never changes. We either accept it or reject it to create our own standard of living. That is why it is so important to seek the truth of God in everything we do.

God is not the "touchy-feely" god that has now become acceptable. . He still expects us to do the best we can. We make excuses for ourselves and for others rather than strive for excellence. It took me many years to understand the parable of the talents (Matthew 25:14) in which Jesus talks of the master who gives one servant five talents, to another two talents, and to another one talent. In the first place, it is difficult to understand why all three men were not given the same number of talents. That is what would seem to be fair to us. However, in spite of what seems to be unfair to us, we are told by this parable that the two men who did something to increase their talents were rewarded, and the third man with only one talent, who hid his money, lost everything. The master called him a lazy servant. What does God expect from us? He expects us to use whatever opportunities, talents, or gifts that we have been given, in a productive manner.

Why do we let our children think there is nothing wrong with sex outside of marriage? How many children are raised in broken homes with a single parent or, as in so many cases, a mother with a live-in boyfriend? What kind of message do our children receive from the garbage they see on television and in the movies? We try to tell ourselves we don't know what to do, and hopefully, they will eventually turn out all right, but chances are great that they will go through a lot of unnecessary suffering in the meantime. When we remove God from their lives, what basis do we have for teaching them right from wrong when we know our authority comes from God?

What is causing all the hostility and hatred, not only in America, but all over the world? It is certainly not Christianity. It is those who hate Christianity, who hate the laws of God. Christianity tells us to love our neighbor as ourselves, not just the neighbor who agrees with us, or makes us feel good, or can do us some good. We are to love all neighbors, even those we don't like. To love our neighbor does not mean we must excuse sin. Sin is real. Evil is real. We would like to think otherwise, but what we think does not change what is.

We are becoming a world of people who have convinced themselves that we are good, loving people, but the hatred I hear from some of us makes me want to cry. I am past being angry. I am worried about what we are becoming. Why do we hate each other? Can it be that we are leaving God out of our lives and letting Satan in? Satan hates Jesus Christ. He hates Christianity. Please give the idea some thought.

God did not create the world without a plan. It is because of our disobedience to His plan that we find ourselves in the pain and suffering that surrounds us. In the beginning, God created a perfect world, and we have been told since the very beginning that a perfect and holy God cannot condone sin. We have reached a time when we no longer take God seriously. We do not want to believe that the troubles we encounter may be the consequences of the seeds we have sown. We do not want to believe in the sacrifice made by Jesus Christ for forgiveness of our sins, so that we would be given the opportunity to live with God eternally. The message of Jesus is love, humility, truthfulness, loyalty, honesty, unselfishness, commitment, compassion, self-discipline, and self-denial. The message of Satan is hatred, self-centeredness, pride, dishonesty, greed, selfishness, and absolutely no self-discipline.

In my search for the truth, I have read the writings of both conservative and liberal authors and journalists. It has been very difficult for me to understand why many of our clergy have turned against their traditional Christian religion. After doing my best to digest the information with an open mind, I am inclined to believe that liberal clergy who call themselves Christians no longer believe the teachings of Christianity. They believe in a new and revised Christianity. Their Christianity has a new set of rules, a twisting and turning of the things Jesus said. In this new Christianity, there would have been no reason for Jesus Christ to have suffered and died. The problem with their reasoning is that without the reason that Jesus suffered, died, and rose on the third day, there would be no Christianity.

Liberal Christians do believe there is a better way, and they believe it is up to them to make this world a better place, to improve the human condition. The message of Jesus to His clergy and to His followers is to save souls for eternity. Liberal clergy have given a new meaning to the role of religion. Their mission is now to promote social justice, and in some cases, to redistribute wealth from the rich to benefit the less fortunate. Social justice is a noble cause, as long as it does not infringe on the liberties of someone else. Jesus did not tell us that we can take from one to give to another. His social gospel is that we are to love our neighbors as ourselves. Each individual heart is being called to have compassion for his neighbor.

Jesus tells us that He wants to be the most important part of our lives, and that He has sent the Holy Spirit to guide us through this life, if we let Him. *"For whoever loses his life for me will find it. What good will it be for a man if he gains the whole world, yet forfeits his soul?"* (Matt. 16:26). Jesus does not force Himself on anyone. We are free to choose whatever we want to believe. It is political correctness that is forced on us.

Christianity tells us something that no other religion tells us. C.S. Lewis explains it very well:

> *The Christian Way - - - The Christian says, 'Creatures are not born with desires unless satisfaction for those desires exists. "*
>
> *(Mere Christianity 136).*

> *If I find in myself a desire which no experience in this world can satisfy, the most probable explanation is that I was made for another world. If none of my earthly pleasures satisfy it, that does not prove that the universe is a fraud. Probably earthly pleasures were never meant to satisfy it, but only to arouse it, to suggest the real thing.*
>
> *(Mere Christianity 136-137).*

Liberal clergy no longer seem to be concerned with saving souls for the promised eternal life in heaven through Jesus Christ. Their main concern is a man-devised social gospel. Some do not believe Jesus is God, nor do they believe in the resurrection, yet they call themselves Christians. They do not speak of sin, repentance, or the fact that Jesus died on the cross for our sins. As destructive as their false religion is to their adult followers, it does not compare to what we are allowing them to do to our children.

> *"And if anyone causes one of these little ones who believe in me to sin, it would be better for him to be thrown into the sea with a large millstone tied around his neck."*
> (Mark 9:42)

How Christianity Changed the World

Love the Lord your God with all your heart
and with all your soul and with all your mind,
and love your neighbor as yourself.
Matthew 22:34

Why and how has Christianity changed the world? The *why* question can be easily answered with the truth. Christianity comes from the teachings of Jesus Christ, who is God. Whether you believe His teachings by faith or by reason, a thorough study of the scriptures will prove that these teachings cannot be improved on. The Bible is our instruction manual for a successful and meaningful life. Jesus taught from the Old Testament and the New Testament tells us about His life and His teachings. We cannot go wrong if we follow His instructions. Even though Jesus was the greatest teacher who ever lived, there is a more important explanation as to why He changed the world. He is the only religious leader who has ever died, risen from the dead, and ascended to heaven. He is the only religious leader who has died for our sins and has promised those who believe and trust in Him eternal life in heaven.

I will try to answer the *how* question. Christianity is a life of sacrifice, a life of service, not self-service. As Jesus transformed His disciples and the early Christians, and continues to transform followers to the present time, Christianity had a great impact on a pagan world. It was Christianity that condemned infanticide, child abandonment, abortion, human sacrifices, and suicide, all of which were allowed in the pagan world at that time. The early followers of Jesus were brutally persecuted for spreading His message of love and forgiveness. *"Whoever wants to be great among you must be your servant, and whoever wants to be first must be your slave - - just as the Son of Man did not come to be served, but to serve, and to give his life as a ransom for many." (Matthew 20:26-28)*.

It was Christianity that changed a growing culture of depraved sexual relations by bringing dignity and honor to marriage between a man and a woman, a holy estate instituted by God. Adultery, fornication, public portrayal of sexual activity, prostitution, homosexuality, pedophilia, lesbianism, group sex, and bestiality are all condemned by Christianity. These practices were not seen as morally wrong in the pagan culture that was replaced by Christianity.

Women were highly regarded by Jesus. Many non-Christian practices, both past and present, have little respect or regard for the rights of women or children. These terrible practices in some cultures (and religions) have been condemned by the Christian world. Christianity teaches us that women and men are of equal value with different roles. God asks that women be humble, loving, and understanding wives and mothers. Not all women marry, some are unable to bear children, and some have no desire to bear children, but for the most part, women do desire to marry and have children, and those who do not become wives and mothers will find their calling if they give their lives to Jesus.

Men have a different role to play. Men are asked by God to be humble, loving, and understanding husbands in the image of Jesus, and to be the spiritual leader and breadwinner of the family. This does not give the husband the right to be abusive to his wife. He is to cherish her as she is to cherish him. Whether one's calling is to be wife, mother, husband, father, priest, nun, or single person, it is doing the will of God that brings an inner peace, joy, happiness, and fulfillment. Whatever one's situation is in life, God will make life worthwhile, if one lets Him.

Fairness, as a right, is a liberal idea. Fairness is an ideal we all know should be practiced. Socialism is a failed attempt at fairness. Secular humanists have a hard time dealing with the unfairness in the world, but they also have a hard time dealing with the idea of sin or the delayed justice of God. They believe that, if given a chance, they would succeed in making the world a much better place. The problem with their ideas is that they do not include God. They are man-created, rather than God-created. God calls Himself a God of Justice---no evil will go unpunished; no good will go unrewarded. Justice may not always be visible to us, but it is wise to remember that even though justice may be delayed, it is still justice. God promises us an inner peace and joy if we trust Him. If we do not trust Him, He really owes us nothing.

Compassion is a very important part of Jesus' message. However, it has a deeper meaning than many want to give it. There is a difference between being compassionate because one is truly interested in the welfare of the other person in contrast to being compassionate because one wants to feel better about oneself. One is true compassion; one is self-gratification. It does not help anyone to be told, repeatedly, that he or she is a victim of society. Society is not responsible for the success or failure of anyone. Individuals have certain responsibilities and government has certain responsibilities.

Christianity teaches us that we do not have to be victims, especially in the United States of America. Our society cannot keep anyone from succeeding. The opportunity for a successful life is open to everyone, but it is not a right. We must work hard, and if we want to be truly successful, we must trust God and follow His laws. It is not in the best interest of anyone to be told there are no consequences for offending God and disobeying His laws.

Christian charity is completely voluntary, and anyone who calls himself a Christian and does not have compassion is not a true Christian. Non-Christians, who claim to live a good and decent life without Jesus, have forgotten the origin of goodness and compassion, just as they have forgotten the foundation of the liberty they enjoy in this Judeo-Christian nation.

There seems to be no end to the number of Christian charities that provide food, shelter, and assistance to those in need. Homes for displaced children and homes for the mentally ill were established out of Christian compassion, some of which has now been replaced by government "compassion," but there are still thousands of Christian organizations that help children and those in need. We now have government-sponsored foster homes for displaced children, and homeless people living in the streets because the mental hospitals, where they once lived, have been closed down.

The Red Cross was started by Jean Henri Dunant, whose faith in Jesus Christ was of first importance to him. Before he died, he said, *"I am a disciple of Christ as in the first century, and nothing more."* (How *Christianity Changed the World, Alvin J. Schmidt, p. 266).*

In Christian compassion, he and four associates, together with twenty-four delegates from sixteen nations, formed the International Red Cross in 1864. There was also Florence Nightingale, a Christian who devoted her life to hospital reform and nursing, and Dorothea Dix, another Christian, who worked persistently, and was successful, in improving conditions for the mentally ill. Christianity is the love of Christ for all of us. The Civil Rights Amendment came about because of the Christian belief that all men are created equal. Martin Luther King, who was a great civil rights leader, was a Christian minister. When he said, *"I have a dream that my four little children will one day live in a nation where they will not be judged by the color of their skin but by the content of their character,"* he was preaching a Christian message. (*From the Martin Luther King, Jr. "I Have A Dream" speech delivered on the steps at the Lincoln Memorial in Washington D.C. on August 28, 1963).* It would be good for all of us if this Christian message was taken seriously today by all races.

Secular Humanism / Liberalism / Conservatism

*The wrath of God is being revealed from heaven
against all the godlessness and wickedness of
men who suppress the truth of their wickedness,
since what may be known about God is plain to
them, because God has made it plain to them.*
Romans 1:18

It is becoming more evident everyday that there is a war going on in America. Some call it a cultural war and some call it a war between Christianity and humanism. I call it a war against God, because it is a war between Christianity and atheism. There are definitely two different worldviews. Christianity tells us that the world was created by God, and that God created man in His image, but in his disobedience, man became sinful, and that God the Father sent God the Son to save us from eternal damnation. The humanist worldview tells us that God has nothing to do with our earthly lives. The humanist worldview is divided into many "*isms.*" I have mentioned Secular Humanism and Christian Humanism. Also to be considered are:

Marxim (socialism), the theory developed by Karl Marx and Frederick Engles, which advocates the system of the production of goods by society (community) rather than by private individuals so that all members of society may share in the work, the product, and the profits.

Leninism (communism) is another humanistic worldview that has its beginning with a type of socialism, but results in ruthless suppression of all opposition political parties and suppression of individual liberties under a disctatorship.

The New Age Movement is another worldview which has various beliefs, depending on the New Age follower's own sense of right and wrong. This movement is made up of different religions, such as Buddhism, Zen Sufism, Taoism, Gnosticism, etc. Most followers will agree, however, that all humanity, indeed all life, everything in the universe is spiritually interconnected, participating in the same energy. God is one name for that energy. (Wikepedia, the free encyclopedia).

It is also evident that more Christians are drawn to conservatism and more humanists are drawn to liberalism. It is ironic that both conservatives and liberals both believe that they must take America back. In spite of the idea in today's world that everything is relative, we have to realize that one side is right and one side is wrong.

Secular humanism seems to have become the popular religion in America, and secular humanism and Islam seem to have the strongest appeal in the world today. What has happened to traditional Christianity and Judaism? A culture of progressiveness (liberalism) has become very popular. I see liberal Christianity as a religion that does not promote a personal relationship with God and that somehow misses the Christian message - - - nor does it mention the holiness of God and the destructiveness of sin, and that Jesus Christ died for our sins. C.S. Lewis writes:

> *The central Christian belief is that Christ's death has somehow put us right with God and given us a fresh start. We are told that Christ was killed for us, that His death has washed out our sins, and that by dying He disabled death itself.*
>
> *---- C. S. Lewis,*
> *Mere Christianity 54*

> *Now what was the sort of 'hole' man had gotten himself into? He had tried to set up on his own, to behave as if he belonged to himself. In other words, fallen man is not simply an imperfect creature who needs improvement: he is a rebel who must lay down his arms. Laying down your arms, surrendering, saying you're sorry, realizing that you have been on the wrong track and getting ready to start life over again from the ground floor - - -this movement full speed astern - - - is what Christians call repentance.*
>
> ---- *C. S. Lewis,*
> *Mere Christianity 56*

The liberal message is appealing, exciting, and sounds reasonable. If we eliminate God, or if we change God to an image more to our liking, we may feel better about ourselves for a while, but sooner or later we all have to face the truth. When are we going to experience the paradise that is promised by the humanists? For over two hundred years, we have been hearing about the wonders of socialism and communism, but this form of government has not brought equality to the common man, nor has it brought prosperity. There is no paradise on this earth. This worldview misinforms those who want to believe man is capable of creating a perfect world. The more we hear that we are entitled to a better world, more money, a better lifestyle, etc., we begin to believe someone else is responsible for our well-being. Many people are living in a state of anger because they have not been taught to be self-responsible. The real world does not entitle us to anything. In fact, it is because of Christianity that our founding fathers believed that we have been endowed with a God-given right to life, liberty, and the pursuit of happiness. Other religions do not make such a promise. Humanism makes promises it cannot keep.

After reading the writings of both conservative and liberal authors and journalists, it is my belief, that many liberals, who call themselves Christians, truly believe they are followers of Christ even though they no longer believe that the Bible is the word of God or that tradition has any place in our modern world. What I have found, however, is that these liberal Christians no longer believe the teachings of the traditional religion that has been given to us from the Bible and from tradition. Liberal Christianity circumvents the true message of Jesus:

> *"If anyone would come after me, he must deny himself and take up his cross and follow me. For whosoever loses his life for me will find it. What good will it be for a man if he gains the whole world, yet forfeits his soul?"*
> (Matthew 16:24-26).

Christianity is seen as a religion of rules, of telling other people how they must live their lives. Jesus never forced any rules on anyone, and neither does Christianity. What Christianity does do is to tell us God's purpose for life, the best way to live it, that certain things are expected of us, and that there is a future for us throughout eternity. Evidently, there are some who do not want to hear this message. But, is it in their power to change the reality of the message? If a person is truly interested in finding the truth about life, it would be wise to study the history of Christianity. There is no more beautiful message than the fact that we were created by a God who loves us and wants to share heaven and earth with us.

There was a time when people did not live with the doubts we live with today. It was common knowledge that God created the universe, that He was in charge, that He was our moral authority, and that right and wrong were determined once and for all. Of course, there have always been unbelievers, but they were in the minority, and were not given much credence by the majority. Times have changed. The minority has grown and grown, and now there is a danger that they may become the majority. It is not in the best interest of our children and grandchildren to do nothing. What kind of world are we leaving to our children, and how long will God allow this kind of degeneration to continue?

America has been a great and blessed nation, but we have gone through many changes in our culture during the past forty years, and now we are seeing the results of the seeds we have sown. There is a movement of secular humanism that is slowly removing God from our society. Christian worship of God is becoming more and more unacceptable in public. America has been a blessed nation because the majority of her citizens have tried to live their lives by following Judeo-Christian principles, but as we turn further and further away from God, we must wonder just how long God will continue to bless America.

Secular humanism has slowly been creeping into traditional religion, which has led to the dissension we see today. We now have conservative Christians who believe in the absolute authority of God and liberal Christians who have no belief in absolutes of any kind. The problem is that liberalism has become more socialistic and man-centered and has strayed from holding to the God-given principles that made America a great and blessed nation.

Let us go back to a time when America was a united God-centered country. Liberalim and conservatism were not always fighting words. Franklin D. Roosevelt,, John F. Kennedy, and Hubert H. Humphrey were liberal-conservative Democrats. Our society began to change after 1963. Following the death of President Kennedy, this liberal-conservative balance began to tip toward liberal secularism. God was rejected from the public schools and from public llife, and liberalism became a type of socialistic activism. As many people have said, "*The Democratic Party left us.*"

We have been led to believe that racial equality is a liberal precept. That is not true. In the strict and purest sense, it is conservatism that holds this truth. It was Republican-minded citizens who broke away from the Whigs (who were in huge part followers of Jesus, the Son of God. Therefore, it is not true that liberalism spawned racial equality. The truth by definition and by God's Word is to be conserved.

A problem arises when we stray from the truth. Jesus is Truth.. When we stray from truth, we stray from Jesus. Truth is neither liberal or conservative. It is a person's reaction to the truth that determines it to be one or the other. The problem with liberalism today is that many liberals have aligned themselves with secular humanism. There are no absolutes in secular humanism; accordingly, there is not room for God, for changeless Truth.

It is up to each one of us to find the true answer. There is only one way to know the will of God, and that is a day by day relationship with Him through prayer, penance, and repentance. He will guide us in the right direction and give us the grace we need if we put our complete trust in Him.

Liberalism has been responsible for many changes in our society. Some changes have made the world a better place. Some have created more problems. Good intentions do not always solve problems. Sometimes good intentions create new problems, especially when we make excuses for every human failing. We all have faults and weaknesses. It is God's intention that we push ourselves, with His help, to overcome our faults and weaknesses. It is because of our faults and weaknesses that we are sinful human beings. We can say, *"Then, it's not my fault."* Well, God tells us it is our fault when we do not ask for His help. He has offered us a *new nature* to replace the old nature. *"Rid yourselves of all the offenses you have committed, and get a new heart and a new spirit. Why will you die, O house of Israel? For I take no pleasure in the death of anyone, declares the Sovereign Lord. Repent and live."* (Ezekiel 18: 31-32). When we turn to Jesus to help us in our spiritual growth, we begin to understand the real meaning of life, God's purpose in creating us, and what is expected of us. *"Therefore, if anyone is in Christ, he is a new creation; the old has gone, the new has come.* (2 Corinthians:17)

The message of Jesus to His clergy is to save souls for eternity. Liberal clergy have given a new meaning to the role of religion. Their mission now is to promote social justice, and in some cases redistribute wealth from the rich to benefit the less fortunate. Social justice is a noble cause as long as it does not infringe on the liberties of one person in favor of another.

The problem I see with liberalism is that it is too closely related to secular humanism and to socialism. It is built on the premise that whether or not God exists, we cannot expect or depend on Him to help us in our daily lives. That is exactly the opposite of the Christian message. Liberals, today, seem to believe that it is within our own power and our responsibility to alleviate poverty, pain, and suffering from this world. They do not acknowledge the fact that disobedience to God is a sin, and sin is responsible for much of the suffering in the world. They do not understand the holiness of God and that sin offends His goodness and holiness. If we can eliminate some of our sinful practices, we may eliminate some of our suffering. The liberal solutions sound very good and compassionate. In most cases, the solution is spending more money without properly addressing the problem. After more than thirty-five years of liberal programs, the plight of humanity has shown little improvement.

I see today's liberalism as a secularist religion. Christianity and liberalism are no longer compatible. A true Christian is a follower of Christ in everything, not just His social gospel. Today's liberal may or may not believe in God, but he or she does not believe God. He is the one and only God of creation, who has given us free will to either accept His word or to reject it. Many have chosen to accept the parts of the Bible they agree with, and to reject what they find objectionable. In the name of compassion and tolerance, liberalism has opened the door to all kinds of sin, with expectation of no consequences. The consequences are real. They are responsible for the degeneration of our society.

Liberalism is dangerous because it tends to take us away from God, not towards Him. That is why it will never work. It is a good thing to try to make the world a better place with the help of God; it is folly to think we can do it without Him. I have listened to people on the right and I have listened to people on the left. Both sides have some good arguments, but I am not looking for arguments; I am looking for the truth.

The one thing I know it that God is truth. There is no truth outside of God. I see that there is a difference in the perception of God between liberal Christians and conservative Christians. Conservatives see God as their moral authority. Liberals do not believe in a moral authority. They have their own morality.

Many well-meaning people are unwittingly becoming humanists as they put God in the background and place human beings in the number one position. Many of our religious leaders have also fallen into the trap of secular humanism. God's ways are not easy. St. Matthew writes, *"For wide is the gate and broad the road that leads to destruction, and many enter through it. But small is the gate and narrow the road that leads to life, and only a few find it."* (Matthew 7:13-14).

In fact, the laws of God make life very difficult for us in today's modern world. We expect more than God has promised, we are no longer grateful for what we have, and we take too much for granted, especially our freedom. Those clergy who have turned against the teachings of traditional religion in an attempt to liberate their people from injustices in the world have also put man before God.

There is now a difference of opinion regarding moral values. Just as God is the moral authority of the right, political correctness has become the moral authority of the left. The left does not accept the idea of sin or of good versus evil. Are the Ten Commandments out of date? Do they have a place in government? Revisionist history cannot change truth. It seems to me that the revisionist history that has been imposed on us has encouraged hatred and intolerance because it produces a false picture of reality. My anger with all the revisionist history in both religion and education has changed to sadness. Anger is only useful when it is used for a positive purpose. My anger stems from the rejection of God I have seen over the past forty years. Something happened in the

1960s that has changed the way many Americans feel about religion and about God. That something is a rebellion against the laws of God. We have found that trying to live within the laws of God is not easy. A false doctrine of tolerance is an enabler. It reinforces the belief that the holiness of God is not offended by what we do and that there really is no such thing as sin. Why did Jesus die for our sins if there is no such thing as sin? Are we going to do it our way or are we going to listen to God? Time will tell what legacy we will leave for the next generation.

I have found that the basic truths, taught by the Catholic Church through scripture and tradition handed down from the disciples of Jesus Christ, give us the closest understanding of the true message of God. The Catholic Church was the beginning of the Christian message by the first followers of Christ. There have been many revisions and divisions throughout history, but the basic truths of Christianity remain the same.

Secular humanism contradicts Christianity. A choice must be made by each one of us. We can choose God or we can choose humanism, which is a form of atheism.

America, A Blessed Nation

If my people, who are called by my name, shall humble themselves, and pray and seek my face, and turn from their wicked ways, then I will hear from heaven and forgive them their sin and heal their land.
2 Chronicles 7:14

America is not an accident, just as the universe is not an accident. Both are within the plan of God. For those who choose to believe that the world is a happening by chance, please remember that it is God who has given you the free will to make that choice.

America has been an example of God's grace, and with His help we Americans may, once again, make this country a beacon of light to the rest of the world. Let us ask God to help us fill the moral void created by the Old World's abandonment of the Christian principles on which America was fashioned.

Americans are people who have come from every nation. It is not as if God prefers one race or nationality over another. He calls all people to love Him and to be willing to follow the instructions He has given them. We were a beacon to the world for many years. I am afraid we are not a very bright light today, but I don't think the light is out completely. There is a glimmer, a glimmer of hope, that we can once again be a great nation.

The human race is, and has always been made up of a combination of liberal minded and conservative minded people. The problem we find today is that liberalism has become more socialistic and man-centered than holding to the God-given principles the Fathers of our country relied on.

I don't think God has given up on us yet. But, I have to wonder how long He is going to put up with our disobedience and disregard for the moral and social standards He has given us. How true are we to ourselves and to God? When we look in the mirror, what do we see?

There is a misrepresentation of moral values in our secular world. We are trying to replace God with political correctness. Since political correctness is a man-made morality and does not come from God, it will fall short of its intent. Political correctness may change some minds, but it cannot change the hearts of man. It takes the grace that comes only from God to change our hearts to conform to His will, and courageous dedication on our part.

Without moral values, we cannot have moral leaders, and without moral leaders, we cannot have a united country. Today, we do not have a united country.   In 1778, President Adams said:

> *"We have no government armed with power capable of contending with human passions unbridled by morality and religion.   Avarice, ambition, revenge, or gallantry, would break the strongest cords of our Constitution as a whale goes through a net.   Our Constitution was made for a moral and religious people.   It is wholly inadequate to government of any other."*
>
> *(America's God and Country 10).*

Moral and truly religious people do not lie and deceive others for their own gain or to achieve their agendas.   We find ourselves wondering whom to believe.   Without the truth we are running in circles, not knowing what decisions to make.

We respect and honor the fathers of our country. They were honorable men, who had both integrity and humility. They had a great love and respect for both God and country, and realized that into their hands was given an opportunity to bring into this world a government governed by the laws of the creator or the universe. Although we have had some presidents, members of Congress, and local politicians who have put their own interests before their country's or their constituents', for the most part, we have had some very admirable statesmen. It is very important, if America is to survive *as America,* that we continue to elect statesmen of honesty and integrity.

As we move our country towards a secular humanist nation and we lose the intervention of God, what will become of America? We may not be here to see the results of our disobedience, but what are we leaving to our children and our grandchildren? God has been very patient with us, but we will never win the war against Him.

We expect our leaders to be virtuous, but what about ourselves? It is amazing to realize that our nation was built by men who depended on God for inspiration and direction, and today we are doing everything possible to separate God from our leaders and our government. We cannot have a government of men and women of integrity, humility, and honesty if we are going to eliminate anyone who depends on God for guidance. It was Abigail Adams who wrote, *"A patriot without religion in my estimation is as great a paradox as an honest man without the fear of God. Is it possible that he whom no moral obligations bind, can have any real good will towards men?"* (America's God and Country 3). Without the love for and the fear of God, we will fall under the influence of the devil. We can see it happening before our very eyes.

America is great because America has been blessed by God, because America has been a Judeo-Christian nation, whose laws are based on the laws of God. We Americans have believed for over two hundred years that God is our moral authority and that He has given us perfect moral standards to live by. In today's world, morality does not necessarily mean God's moral standards. For example, the words *good* and *moral* have a different meaning to different people. Liberals will say that being moral means that we are to tolerate everything and everyone (except

Christians). Conservatives believe being moral means to honor and be obedient to the laws of God.

Our desire to do things our own way is taking precedent over the ways of God, and we can see the degeneration of our country. We know something is wrong when only one child in five will grow up in a family with both parents married and living together. I have seen young single mothers trying to make ends meet because of an abusive marriage. I have seen some trying to put some kind of life together with their children and a live-in boyfriend. I have also seen heartbroken men whose wives have walked out for something better. The adults are miserable in these situations, but what about the children?

There has never been such an assault on the family. Families are the foundation of our nation. Race and nationality do not matter. What matters are good and intact families. The breakdown of the family will be the breakdown of the nation. There are many reasons for the breakdown of the family, but disobedience to and disregard for God's laws are the most culpable.

We all have a duty to protect our children and to avoid leading them astray. Our culture is certainly doing a very poor job of keeping our children out of harm's way. Our young people have been taught to expect too much. They have not been properly prepared for the hardships of life. We seem to see little, if anything, wrong with eleven-year-olds having oral sex. I have heard adults (even parents) say that oral sex is safer than having intercourse. What is a child supposed to think when his or her mother sees nothing wrong with her young child experimenting with sex or living in an unmarried sexual relationship?

What about all the sex and violence that our children are exposed to in movies, television, video games, the Internet, etc.? The biggest problem we have is that too many adults see nothing wrong with this, because they don't want to be deprived of watching this filth. It is very difficult to fight this kind of assault on morality and decency as long as so many people want it to continue.

Sex, violence, and vulgarity are what our children see everyday. They are not taught respect for others. They are led to believe that they are in charge, and all too often, they are. With the exception of some very good parents and teachers, who are very dedicated to teaching the children in their care to become responsible adults, we have done a very poor job of raising the next generation. Whatever happened to teaching children to strive for excellence? God expects us to do the best we can with the gifts He has given us, and everyone has some special gift that will be lost if it is not used.

There is no better place than America to succeed. There are countless opportunities for anyone who is willing to learn, to work hard, and to persevere.

Nothing is easy; life is very hard for most people, but please do not waste your time envying those who seem to have it all. In a long run, no one has it all. Millions of people have started with nothing, or very little, and have become great success stories. That is the American dream.

Not everyone will be wealthy, but wealth is not what brings happiness. In fact, many times wealth brings unhappiness, because the person who becomes wealthy does not know how to handle his wealth. Some become greedy and can think of nothing but getting wealthier. Some begin to think they are God, and become so arrogant and prideful that they can never find peace, contentment, or happiness. And some become so self-centered and self-important that they contribute nothing but misery to society. A real American dream would be to become wealthy so that one could use the money to help those who truly need help.

Since the 1960s, there has been a continuous movement to rid America of God. We are at a crossroads in this country. As late as the 1950s, men like President Harry Truman and Supreme Court Justice Earl Warren spoke of the importance of religion in America. President Truman said:

The fundamental basis of this nation's law was given to Moses on the Mount.   The fundamental basis of our Bill of Rights comes from the teachings we get from Exodus and St. Matthew, from Isaiah, and St. Paul.   I don't think we emphasize that enough these days.   If we don't have proper fundamental moral background, we will finally end up with a totalitarian government which does not believe in rights for anybody except the State."

(Reclaiming America for Christ 22).

In 1954, Earl Warren stated:

I believe no one can read the history of our country without realizing that the Good Book and the Spirit of the Savior have from the beginning been our guiding geniuses. Whether we look to the first charter of Virginia or to the Charter of New England, or to the Charter of Massachusetts Bay, or to the Fundamental Orders of Connecticut, the same objective is present. A Christian government of Christian principles.

I believe the entire Bill of Rights came into being because of the knowledge our forefathers had of the Bible and their belief in it: freedom of belief, of expression, of assembly, of petition, the dignity of the individual, the sanctity of the home, equal justice under the law, and the reservation of power to the people. I like to believe that we are living today in the spirit of the Christian religion. I like also to believe that as long as we do so, no great harm can come to our country.

---- Earl Warren,
Time Magazine, February 15, 1954

There is no doubt as to what the great leaders of America believed throughout the history of this country. There is also no doubt that we have gone through a period of revisionist history, and much of our true history has been left out of the textbooks that our children are being taught from. Social engineering and political correctness have replaced truth in many cases.

Jesus said, *"Any kingdom divided against itself will be ruined, and a house divided against itself will fall."* (Luke 11:17). Until the 1960s, we were a nation united. We are in danger of becoming a house divided among itself: some who believe in a God-centered nation and some who believe in a man-centered nation. Those who are secularists insist that Christianity would take away all our liberties. There can be nothing further from the truth.

Freedom From Religion

Congress shall make no law respecting an establishment
of religion, or prohibiting the free exercise thereof; or
abridging the freedom of speech, or of the press; or
the right of the people peaceably to assemble, and to
petition the Government for a redress of grievances.
The First Amendment of the U.S. Constitution

You will not find it anywhere in the U.S. Constitution, but liberal secularists today are doing their best to convince us that it is unconstitutional to have any mention or display of religion in the public square. There is a cultural war going on in America, and in order for the liberal secularists' agenda to succeed, religion, especially Christianity, must be eliminated. With God out of the picture, these secularists believe they will not be bound by any moral laws, which they believe will interfere with their freedom. At the front of this fight is the UCLA, followed by a group called Americans United for Separation of Church and State, and another advocacy group called People for the American Way.

We hear the phrase "separation of church and state" again and again. Where did this phrase come from?   On January 1, 1802, Thomas Jefferson wrote a letter to the Danbury Baptists in which the following appeared:

Believing with you that religion which lies solely between
Man & his God, that he owes account to none other for his

faith or his worship, that legitimate powers of government reach actions only, & not opinions, I contemplate with sovereign reverence that act of the whole American people which declared that their legislature should 'make no law respecting an establishment of religion, or prohibiting the free exercise thereof,' thus building a wall of separation between Church & State. Adhering to this expression of the nation in behalf of the rights of conscience, I shall see with sincere satisfaction the progress of those sentiments which tend to restore to man all his natural rights, convinced he has no natural right in opposition to his social duties.

----- *(Jefferson's Letter to the Danbury Baptists),*
LC Information Bulletin, June 1998).

It would seem that Jefferson was confirming that government cannot prohibit free exercise of religion, nor can government establish a national or state religion. There are arguments on both sides. I am afraid there is a movement by secularists and atheists today, who would like to remove all aspects of God, and especially Christianity, from our society.

The following is taken from *Wikipedia:*

"The phrase "separation of church and state" does not appear in the Constitution, but rather is derived from a letter by Thomas Jefferson to a group identifying themselves as Danbury Baptists, dated January 1, 1802. In that letter, Jefferson uses the term 'wall of separation between Church and State' to show the Danbury Baptists that in both Connecticut and the entire U.S., religious freedom is an inalienable right that government cannot take away.

----- *Wikipedia, The Free Enclyclopedia*
(Also see Supreme Court Case 43 U.S. 1275;
1844 U.S. Lexis 323; IIL.)

The attack on religion is being made on many different fronts, but the Left has been most successful in the public schools. Even though the ACLU has lost many of their lawsuits, the very threat of being sued has encouraged many school administrators to do away with any resemblance of anything religious, rather than face the possibility of a lawsuit. Choosing the public schools as a training ground for their agenda has been a wise move for the ACLU; their agenda is the removal of God from public life. What better place is there to begin than with the very young?

Since the 1960s, a series of federal court decisions began to erode the influence on our schools. In the last generation, there have been so many lawsuits against school-sponsored religious activities that the belief that all religious influence must be removed from our public schools has prevailed. While some state-mandated religious practices have been held unconstitutional, even in these court opinions, the value, and even necessity, of religious content in the public school curriculum has been stated. The American culture has been shaped by the Bible, and if we take all religion out of our public life, we will change the American culture.

In his book, *A War Against Christmas*, John Gibson cites case after case in which school administrators have chosen to abandon all symbols of Christmas, even those such as Santa Claus and the Christmas tree, which are considered to be secular. In most cases, the fear of a lawsuit is responsible for these decisions. We are all so confused today, we do not know what to believe anymore.

In the late 1970s, the Sioux Falls School District adopted a guideline to govern secular and religious holidays. In an effort to be fair, yet adhere to the U.S. Constitution, the school policy allowed the use of religious symbols (including religions other than Christianity), but indoctrination of any religion was prohibited. This was not good enough for Roger Florey, a parent who, in an attempt to remove the use of any religious symbols, filed a lawsuit against the school district, claiming that the school policies and practices violated the U.S. Constitution. The school board policy was upheld. (Florey v Sioux Falls School District, 619 F. 2d 1311 (1980).

In 1925, it was the ACLU that brought about the Scopes Monkey Trial. In an effort to undermine religious entities that believed in the inerrancy and authority of the Bible, the ACLU advertised for a teacher who would be willing to challenge the Butler Act, which prohibited the teaching of evolution in the public schools in Tennessee. (Scopes v State, 152 Tenn. 424, 278 S.W. 57 (Tenn.) 1925).

One lawsuit after another has been brought about trying to remove any form of Christian symbols from public life. The Left has not been as interested in interfering with other religions' symbols for the present time. It is Christianity that has to go, as far as these organizations are concerned. Most of the cultural elite, who are in positions of power and in control of education and the media, are anti-Christian, if not also anti-religion. Their argument is that Christianity is intolerant, judgmental, and offensive. Their hypocrisy is evident, as their political correctness becomes intolerance in the name of tolerance. It is the belief of these secularists that if God is removed from our society, the very idea of sin will also be removed. They also hate authority of any kind. They want to believe that they are free to do whatever they please, even though they do not offer this freedom to everyone.

The history of the ACLU is very interesting, and somewhat surprising. The American Civil Liberties Union has very few "American" interests behind it. The founder of the ACLU was Roger Baldwin, who was an agnostic and a socialist. It is no surprise to me that the mindset of much of the ACLU is that only a small group of intellectuals have the capability of understanding and dictating what everyone else should believe. Former ACLU president, Norman Dorsen, explained, "Baldwin thought of the ACLU as a group of elitists, of highly educated people, a few thousand at most throughout the country, who would be the vanguard of a movement to protect individual rights in this society." *(The ACLU vs. America 8)*. Baldwin also believed he had the right to decide who would be allowed into the ACLU and who would be rejected. His reasoning was that the ACLU was a private organization.

(The ACLU vs. America 8).   It is ironic that the same ACLU, today, would call this discrimination.

In his Harvard University class book, Roger Baldwin wrote, *"I am for socialism, disarmament, and ultimately the abolishing of the state itself as an instrument of violence and compulsion.   I seek social ownership of property, the abolition of the propertied class, and sole control of those who produce wealth.   Communism is the goal."*

(The ACLU vs. America 13), (Discoverthenetwork.org., Roger Baldwin 2). The goal of the ACLU is to change America from a Judeo-Christian nation to a secular nation by removing any vestige of religious faith and also the traditional family from the public square.

In *The ACLU vs. America,* I found the following:

> *This mind set that the ACLU knows what's best for the great unwashed masses, drives the ACLU's disdain for the will of the people.   This mind-set also is behind its use of the judiciary, rather than the electorate, to implement its agenda. In addition, the promotion of 'individual rights' ultimately results in a society in which the right of individuals drastically outweigh the collective responsibility individuals should have to society or the concepts of a higher law or duty individuals are responsible to follow.   The result is a modernistic, media-driven, self-centered society that has evolved to "all about me" instead of "all about us." a nation that no longer, in too many instances, lives up to the challenge of our late President John F. Kennedy: 'Ask not what your country can do for you, ask what you can do for your country'.*
> *- - Alan Sears and Craig Osten,*
> *The ACLU vs. America 8,9*

The American Civil Liberties Union and Planned Parenthood work hand in hand. The history of Planned Parenthood is also very interesting. This organization was started by Margaret Sanger, an atheist and avowed socialist, blaming the evils of contemporary capitalism for the unsatisfactory conditions of the young working-class women.   She also believed in eugenics, a pseudo science claiming that human heredity traits can be improved through social intervention. (*Wikipedia, the free enclyclopdia*). In her attempt to improve the conditions for women, Margaret Sanger inadvertently opened the door to more pain and unhappiness for women. Sexual promiscuity and abortion on demand have become acceptable by most in our society. The message being sent to our children and teenagers is something we should all be concerned about.

There is a very important and basic difference in the interpretation of morality among conservative Christians, liberal Christians and humanists. Conservative Christians believe in a law-based morality. Since our Founding Fathers based our laws on God's laws, liberal Christians and humanists find it necessary to rely on activist judges to change the laws to meet their standards.

For the left, morality is relative rather than absolute. An example of Christian Humanism or liberal Christianity is Bishop John Shelby Spong who calls himself a Christian who finds the idea that Jesus died for our sins offensive. He writes, *"Jesus died for our sins" has become not just unbelievable but bizarre to modern ears. (The Substitution by Death of Jesus on the Cross Brings Salvation, Part III, John Shelby Spong, June 15, 2007).*

For the conservative Christian, morality means following the laws of God in the belief that God has given us a perfect standard to live by. Sin is the deliberate rejection of God's laws, sin separates us from Him, and the wages of sin is death. Because God loves us, our sins are forgiven through the death of Jesus Christ if we are truly repentant.

Because we have fallen into humanism of all types, many do not believe they are doing anthing wrong or rejecting God's laws, nor do they give much thought to whether or not heaven and hell really exist. I do not know how God will deal with those who do not know, but it seem obvious to me that we are all reaping the consequences of each others' sins.

Liberal Christians and humanists consider individual rights to be more important than personal responsibility. They insist on the right to liberty, but in order to achieve their goals, they give us more laws, which actually take away freedom in the name of freedom.

The liberal secularists have done a very good job of convincing many people that they are on the side of the little guy, and that they are fighting for the rights of the average person. In reality, they are fighting against God and the laws of God. They want to do away with the idea of a moral authority so that they can change the laws in the name of tolerance, diversity, and acceptability of sinful acts. As far as they are concerned, the only sinful acts are those of Christians or Orthodox Jews. There is no evil and there are no sins, except those that do not agree with their agenda. The ACLU claims they are fighting for the civil rights of the American people, and in many cases they do. However, their agenda is that there is such a separation between church and state that the name of God or anything pertaining to the Judeo-Christian God is unconstitutional, even though there is nothing in the Constitution that forbids the reference to God in the public square. God is not a religion. God is the creator of the universe.

Secularists believe they do not want or need God in their lives. Their reasons may differ, but basically it is their pride that takes over the place of their humility. Some want power, some want the freedom to do as they please, some believe God is not doing enough to help the less fortunate - - and the list goes on. The mistake liberal secularists make is that God knows what He is doing, His laws cannot be replaced, and He is the one in power. He has the power to get rid of us if He chooses; we cannot rid the world of God.

It is Christianity and Orthodox Judaism that liberals are afraid of, because Christians and Orthodox Jews are the people who are trying to follow the laws of God. These are the people who accept the words of the Bible as God's truth. Christians accept Jesus Christ as Lord, and the Orthodox Jews accept the teachings of the Old Testament. Liberal secularists reject both God and the Bible.

I am convinced that it is the excessive sin in the world that is causing so much unhappiness. I have lived a long time and I remember a much different world. There has always been sin in the world, but Americans have always fought against evil. Now we have Americans who are condoning evil. If the secularists are allowed to win this war against God, it will destroy our American heritage and culture. Our present laws are not on the side of the liberal secularists in many cases so they must depend on left-leaning activist judges to rule in their favor. Their main issues, besides Christianity, are abortion, civil rights, and the environment, but they do not always present an honest argument. They claim to be fighting for fairness and justice, but their standards vary, depending on the circumstances. In the case of abortion, they will fight for the civil rights of the mother who is about to murder her unborn child, but they refuse to acknowledge the civil rights of the child whose right to be born has been taken away.

The war is on between the people who want God in their lives and those who do not, and there will be no joy or peace in the world until we, like the Israelites, come back to Him. If America is to continue being the great country we love, we must continue fighting those who wish to destroy what so many of our brave men and women have fought and died for. Rather than excluding all religion from the public square, would it not be better, in the name of fairness, to include all religions?

Poverty in America

He who oppresses the poor shows contempt for their
Maker, but whoever is kind to the needy honors God.
Proverbs 14:31

He who ignores discipline comes to poverty and shame,
but whoever heeds correction is honored.
Proverbs 13:18

There has to be a better way to solve the problem of poverty in America. Whatever we have been doing for the past forty-five years is not working. In fact, if we consider the situation honestly, we have to admit that we may have done more harm than good. We have produced a culture of dependency. My hope is that we may break the cycle of dependency in the next generation. We must reach the children who are living in poverty, and help them to believe that there is a promising future for them if they will do their best in school, and help them to believe that God loves them and wants the best for them. Many of these children do not get encouragement or moral guidance from their family or social environment. If we really want to help them, we must find a way to reach them. Let's start at the beginning and try to resolve some of these problems.

We first have to take a good and honest look at who the people in poverty are, and understand why they are in the situations they are in. Some are mentally or physically handicapped. Children with special needs must be educated and taken care of. Due to various problems that arise within families, there are times when there is not enough money to support the family, and in these cases, there should be a temporary safety net. There is no question that these people must be helped by both government and private charities.

My hope is that, with God's help, we can find a way to reduce poverty by convincing young people to take advantage of the educational system available to everyone in America, so that they will be self-reliant. Depending on a welfare system, in my opinion, promotes dependency rather than encouragement in self-determination to better oneself. I truly believe we must reach the children before they begin to believe there is no other way for them.

Human nature does not always work in our best interests. If we are given money for doing nothing, we tend to forget that it is in doing something worthwhile, i.e., working for financial means or volunteering for service in a number of ways, that we feel as if we have accomplished something. There is no job so menial that it will not produce a feeling of accomplishment and satisfaction when it is done well. In a misguided effort to be compassionate, we sometimes take away the incentive and initiative that would produce positive results. These children need a good educational system. A good education means that the truth must be taught, rather than political correctness or revisionist history. It is important for every healthy and able child to be taught as soon as he or she is able to understand that every person is responsible for himself or herself. Nothing in this world is free, and if it is given to you free of charge, someone had to pay for it. It does nobody any good to keep telling people, young or old, that they are victims of a country that does not care about them. America offers each one of us the opportunity to do the best we can with our lives, no matter what our race or religion is.

I am not in favor of the idea of multiculturalism in America. I do not like to see Americans hyphenated. We are not helping our children by separating them. They are all Americans, and whether they come from a black or white family living in poverty or a black or white middle-class family, the opportunity to succeed must be available to all. More money is being spent on public education than ever before, but problems with public education persist. Responsible and dedicated parents and teachers must get involved in the proper education of our children.

Parents are a child's first teachers. No one is more important in shaping a child's life than his or her mother and father. It is the parents duty to teach their children the importance of honesty, integrity, and a strong moral character, and to see that they receive a good education. The incentive to learn comes from the parents. In addition to good parents, it takes dedicated teachers who inspire their students, so that they will know the feeling of accomplishment when they put their minds and hearts into learning. A good and moral society also plays a part in instilling proper traits in a child.

Something has gone terribly wrong with our educational system since the 1960s. I can truthfully tell you that before the Great Society came into being, I received my grammar school education in a very poor lower-class neighborhood in Chicago. The neighborhood was a mixture of many races and nationalities, as were the children I went to school with. We were black, white, and whatever. I still remember a boy of Filipino decent named Pacifico, who was always at the head of the class. It was probably because he studied harder than anyone else. (In those days, there was competition, and we were all told to strive for excellence). To this day, I remember my teachers and the positive attitude they inspired in me. The neighborhood may have been poor, and the school may have been poor, but we were blessed with good teachers who inspired us to always do the best we could.

There is no easy road for most of us in this world. We cannot spend our lives envying and vilifying those who were born into wealth. The opportunity to succeed is America's greatest promise. The opportunity, today, is open to everyone, but there is one limitation. The limitation is no longer race, sex, or nationality. The limitation is lack of a skill and an ambition to achieve it. God has given everyone some gift or talent, and He expects it to be expended. A person who has no skill to offer cannot expect someone to offer him a job that requires skill or knowledge.

An improved educational system will reduce poverty. Before it can be accomplished, though, we must examine the problems. The decay in moral values has damaged the education of our children as well as the work-ethic in our society. Man-made political correctness and *self-esteem* curricula have replaced God-given moral standards. As worthwhile as feelings are, they are not more important than the realities of life, such as genuine ego and a strong sense of what can be accomplished with determined effort. Modern educators have forgotten that children can be taught to master these realities of life.

Political correctness retards the process. In trying to make all children feel good about themselves, educators did away with competition, rewards and punishments. And they tempered the grading system. Instead of Gold Stars for hard work and real learning, there were Gold Stars for everyone, or no Gold Stars for anyone. Equality and *self-esteem* were the goal rather than equality of opportunity. (See *Dumbing Down Our Kids, p. 71, Charles J. Sykes).* Weakness in authority was the principal reason behind the breakdown in discipline. New and strange methods of teaching were tried. And they failed. Children did not feel better about themselves, and many were left confused and functionally illiterate. The consequence was a major change in the American work-ethic whereby we saw the installation of false belief: that hard work, self-discipline, and responsibility are not critically important beause we are all entitled to a successful life.

Entitlements were not what my parents had in mind when they, and thousands of other immigrants with little or nothing, came to America.. They could not speak English, but their first priority was to get a job, and the second was to learn English. They worked very hard, for little money, as did all Americans who were lucky enough to have a job. They were grateful to God for what they had, but times were very hard. There was the Depression and most men were out of work. Then there was World War II, and most men had to go to war. Life was hard then; life is hard now.

Life has always been hard. The one thing everyone had was faith and hope for the future. The future is here, but there seems to be little faith or hope left. We are missing the spirit of a God-centered society. Political correctness will never give us what we had in the past.

Every child, no matter what race or nationality, must be taught the importance of studying, learning, and getting a good education. They must also be taught to be honest, to do the very best job they are capable of doing, and to respect themselves and others. If we can change their vision to a hopeful future, rather than one of hopelessness, we may be able to make a dent in the problem of poverty. These children must not feel defeated before they even have a chance to get started.

We have become an "I-have-a-right-to" nation. What do I have a right to? Our Declaration of Independence states, "a right to life, liberty, and the pursuit of happiness." The American people are very compassionate and very generous - - probably the most generous in the world. However, compassion and generosity that is not humbly and gratefully received will not be continued. Resentment will set in if compassion and generosity is expected, rather than appreciated.

I don't see how anything positive can be accomplished as long as so-called leaders keep inciting people, using past injustices, to keep the anger, self-pity, and racism alive. The people and the government in America have acknowledged the injustices of the past, and many Americans, both black and white, fought and died for justice and freedom for all. The Civil Rights movement could not have been won without both white and black people working together. The rabble-rousing has to stop. There will always be some, no matter what race, religion, or worldview, who will continue to complain about whatever cause they can find, but hopefully, the truth will bring us together as Americans in one America

Again, only education and truth can resolve any of the problems that face us. Discrimination of any kind is against the law. Opportunity is open to every American. There is no free lunch. We all have to pay, one way or another, for everything we receive. We have been throwing money at the poverty problem for over forty years and, to date, no one is satisfied. The conservatives complain that we are not dealing with the real problem of poverty, and the liberals complain that we are not spending enough money. The only way the problem will ever be solved is if we all work together, with an honest resolve to find a real solution. There are many on welfare who should not be there because they are capable of working, or would be if they were properly educated. If the able-bodied were responsible for their own welfare, there would be enough money to take care of the disabled and those who truly cannot be completely responsible for their own welfare.

We must deal with the real reason people are living in poverty before we can do anything. The main excuse we hear is that there are no jobs. I will accept the fact that some jobs do not pay very well, but in our economy there are jobs. There is the problem of teenage mothers, unwed mothers, and single mothers. There are problems that deal with drugs and alcohol. The problems must be addressed with something other than political correctness. We must mix compassion and love with discipline. Contrary to political correctness, God tells us we must have self-control and self-discipline if we are to live a successful life.

Even though there are some who want to be responsible for themselves, there are also some who are irresponsible, who do not want to work, and who are happy to take advantage of the system. We know that church-based schools and missions have helped children and adults who have no hope, but we hear protests against faith-based institutions. Why not help these religious institutions help the poor? Would it not be a good idea to help those who truly minister to those who need help?

God Knows Why

*The Spirit Himself testifies with our spirit that we are
God's children. Now if we are children, then we are heirs
- - heirs of God and co-heirs with Christ, if indeed we
share in His sufferings in order that we may share in His
glory. Consider that our present sufferings are not worth
comparing with the glory that will be revealed in us.*
Romans 17:16-18

There are times when I wish I had the power to make everyone happy. However, I have to face reality. I ask myself why God allows so much pain and suffering, yet I remember that life was not always like this. I remember a time when life was enjoyable. Pain and suffering have always been a part of the human condition, but most of us depended on God to get us through the hard times, and He did. He brought us victoriously through the Great Depression and World II. Although everyone I knew was struggling to make ends meet, we were grateful for what we had, and we believed in a better future.

Today, we have more material things than anyone could ask for, but there is very little happiness in this world. It seems that the more we have, the more we want, and expect. We are never satisfied. The hostility, dishonesty, and ingratitude seem to be increasing everyday. It seems that so many are no longer grateful to God for what He has given to them. We seem to have lost the courtesy of listening to the other person's point of view. Personal integrity, moral character, and honesty no longer seem to matter. We all look for these values in the other person, but what about ourselves? This is certainly not true of everyone, but there are enough disgruntled, dishonest, and morally bankrupt people around to cause problems for everyone.

God loves us - - you and me. Because He loves us, He wants the best for us, and because He knows that sin will destroy us, He hates sin. Those who encourage us to sin by telling us that God loves us as we are and that we do not have to change our sinful ways are not doing us any favors. They are actually helping us move towards our destruction. A good father does not encourage his son to commit suicide, and our Father in heaven knows He must discipline us so that we will turn to Him, away from our sinful ways, before we destroy ourselves.

There is no greater mystery, outside of God, than the mystery of life. God gives us life, love, and truth. There is nothing more important. Yet, in this modern world, many no longer search for the truth of God. In our arrogance and pride, we think we are capable of assessing all knowledge by ourselves, without the help of God. This is not what God has planned for us. He did not create us to live without Him.

C. S. Lewis writes:

> "God designed the human machine to run on Himself. He Himself is the fuel our spirits were designed to burn, or the food our spirits were destined To feed on. There is no other. That is why it is just no good asking God to make us happy in our own way without bothering about religion. God cannot give us a happiness and peace apart from Himself, because it is not there. There is no such thing.
> (Mere Christianity 50).

He writes further,

> "Some fatal flaw always brings the selfish and cruel people to the top, and it all slides back into misery and ruin. In fact, the machine conks. It seems to start up all right and

runs a few yards, and then it breaks down. They are trying to run on the wrong juice. That is what Satan has done to humans."

(Mere Christianity 50).

I don't think I would be too far out of line if I were to say that every one of us, at one time or another, has wondered if God really loves us, or if He is cruel, or if He just doesn't care. God is none of these things, but the world (Satan) is all of them. There is a difference. The world does not care if we pray, or if we love it, or if we seek its guidance, but God does care about all of these things. God created us because He wanted to have a loving relationship with us. He wants us to depend on Him, and He wants to hear from us every day.

Does God answer our prayers? This is a question we have all asked, but there is another question to be asked: do we answer God? This is a two-way affair. God has given us life, with certain requests. One of His requests is that we keep in touch. God does not ask any more of us than we are willing to give Him. We each have to decide, with the free will He has given us, what we want to do with our lives.

I have learned through many years of trying to understand God that His gifts do not come in large packages. His gifts come slowly, a little at a time, and in small packages. Sometimes the package is so small that we do not even recognize it as a gift until sometime later.

In this day and age, we are more concerned with finding ourselves than we are with finding God, yet it is in finding God that we find ourselves, and the meaning and purpose of our lives. It is not God's fault if we are dissatisfied with what He desires to give us, because He knows it is for our good, or that we are unable to get everything we feel we are entitled to. Are we really entitled to more than God has promised?

God knows what is good for us and what will do us harm. We can see what happens to some people who have more money than they know what to do with. It is not the money that is harmful. It is their pride that chases out their humility. We cannot accept what God offers us without humility. Pride gets in the way, and tells us whatever God gives us is not enough.

If we are blessed with more money than we know what to do with, God tells us to share some of it with the poor and the unfortunate, and to help those who truly cannot help themselves, through no fault of their own. This is not liberalism. This is Christianity. Jesus does not tell those who have little that they are entitled to take what they need from those who have much. Taking what is not yours is stealing. Stealing is a sin. However, keeping everything you have to yourself is greed. Greed is also a sin. He asks us to be honest and also generous. Sometimes money is not the answer. We are also asked to spread the message of God's gift of salvation, His love, and concern for all men and women, to all nations. God always answers the prayers of those who love Him.

Some may have a problem believing that Adam and Eve were actually the first people of God's creation, but the moral of the story cannot be denied. God created a perfect world with provisions and prohibitions. He has provided us with all the necessities of a good life, and He has made it very clear that in order to enjoy that good life, there are certain actions that are prohibited. When we disobey the rules, we will face the consequences.

If we believe God exists, then we must believe Satan exists also, because it is God who has revealed the truth of Satan's existence to us, and it is Jesus who confirms this truth. When we realize who Satan is and the power he has, we can begin to understand the evil in this world. Evil is the result of disobedience to God. Satan was the first to turn against God; then, he convinced Eve and Adam that God was really no different than they were, and that they were entitled to know everything and to do as they wished. Their decision, and ours, to disobey God is what has brought evil into the world.

God's message to all of us is the same. He asks for our trust, our faith, our humility, our obedience, and our love. If we give Him our trust, He will do the rest. Does this sound easy? No, it is not easy. Life is hard. Life is a long process of learning, and many times that learning process can be painful. The sad story is that without pain, we usually do not learn much. An easy life does not create moral character, nor does it encourage us to seek God. Why would we need God when we have everything we want?

Life has a purpose for each one of us, and it is through the fulfillment of this purpose that we find fulfillment in our lives. We do not find happiness and fulfillment through an easy life, although we may find temporary comfort and pleasure. It is the presence of God in our lives that brings us happiness and fulfillment.

You may ask, "Why didn't God create a perfect world? Well, He did. But, in a perfect world, everything has to be perfect, and that would include us. God chose to give us free will so that we could either choose Him or reject Him. It is God's will that we seek His will. He does not force Himself on us. He asks for our love and trust, but the choice is ours. We have the freedom to do as we will, but there are serious consequences to every sinful act. As difficult as it may sound, we must fight against our own human nature. The good news is that God has promised to help us in this fight. Our human nature tends to believe the lies of Satan. We have the ability, with the grace of God through prayer, to turn from our human nature to our spiritual nature.

God's ways are hard. I know this to be a fact. I also know that His ways are the only way we can find the peace and joyful heart Jesus promised. The evil one has a way of convincing us that our ways are better than God's. There are many things we do not understand. There is nothing that God does not know or understand. We fool ourselves if we think we know more than God or that He does not matter in our decisions. God does test our faith. Nothing is more important in this life than a growing faith in God. He does not give us more than we can bear, because he sheds his strength and grace on those who trust in Him.

We are told to love God with all our heart and to worship and glorify Him. It is not because He needs us to tell Him how wonderful He is. We must honor and glorify God so that we do not honor and glorify ourselves. This is an act of humility on our part.

As a society, we are falling further and further away from God, because that is what we are choosing to do. He has made Himself known to us. He has given us the rules to live by, but we are paying little or no attention to what is asked of us. God is merciful, God is just, and God is serious. We seem to forget that God is holy and He is perfect.

Just as God does not change, there is a moral standard that does not change. Not one of us can measure up to that perfect moral standard. We all fall short of perfection, and we all commit sins against God in one way or another. I may not think life is fair, and I am certain no human being does, but that is the way it is. We are all sinners. Some sins are worse than others, but it is our sins and transgressions that bring on most of our hardships. There are other reasons for the pain and suffering that we experience in this world, but this discussion is about the pain we are responsible for.

Life can be beautiful, but life is not easy. We have learned a great deal during the past forty years. We have tried permissiveness and liberalism, liberating ourselves from the laws of God. The results are disastrous. Children in their teenage and pre-teenage years think there is nothing wrong with experimenting with sex. There is a breakdown in moral character, as well as in our marriages and families. We have lost sight of the really important things in life. Our children no longer live in a wholesome environment. In most cases, it is what we do when we break the laws of God that bring us our pain and misery.

Each one of us will have to face God one day. To those who do not believe God exists, there is nothing I can say. To those who do believe God exists, I will say that a person must be humble in order to know God and to ask for wisdom. Pride stands in the way of knowing and loving God.

"Consider it pure joy, my brothers, whenever you face trials of many kinds, because you know that the testing of

your faith develops perseverance.   Perseverance must finish its work so that you may be mature and complete not lacking anything.   If any of you lacks wisdom, he should ask God, who gives it generously to all without finding fault, and it will be given to him."

(James 1:2-5)

Thy Will Be Done

Our Father, who art in heaven, Hallowed be thy name,
Thy Kingdom come, Thy will be done on earth as it is
in heaven. Give us this day our daily bread and lead
us not into temptation, but deliver us from evil. Amen.
The Lord's Prayer

God did not leave us with no way of finding Him. He desires to be a part of your life and mine. In His wisdom, Jesus Christ compressed into a few words the perfect prayer to Our Father. This prayer embodies the petitions necessary for a fulfilling, spiritual life. A life, if we choose to conform to God's will that will lead us to God and to a meaningful and purpose-filled life.

If you would like to belong to God's family, the Lord's Prayer is a good place to start. God does have a family, and He does invite every person to be a part of this family, but not everyone accepts His invitation. When Jesus gave us the Lord's Prayer, He gave us a pattern for life. The important things we have to know are embodied in this prayer.

When we pray the Our Father, we acknowledge that we have a Father in heaven who created us for Himself and who loves us and wants the very best for us in this life; but more importantly, He wants us to live happily with Him in the next.

We ask that He give us the strength and the grace to live our lives so that His will be done on earth as it is in heaven. We ask that we may have enough to eat each day, and we ask that His grace may lead us away from temptation and that we may be delivered from evil. It is in our best interest to do what God asks, rather than reject His offer and choose to live our lives without Him. It is God's desire to bring each one of us to heaven.

What is the will of God? Every time we pray *the Lord's Prayer*, we ask God for His will to be done on earth. I have always been under the impression that this part of the prayer was a confirmation that God's will would be done some day. However, something Rick Warren said has made me see this in a different light. He writes, "*We live in a fallen world. Only in heaven is everything done perfectly the way God intends. That is why we are told to pray, 'Thy will be done on earth as it is in heaven'.*" *(The Purpose Driven Life, p. 195).* I now see that we are also asking that His will may also be done today. God's will is that each one of us may share eternity with Him in heaven. However, He has also chosen to give us free will. Gregory A. Boyd writes in his book, *Is God To Blame?*, "*Because God desires a creation in which love is a reality, he allows his will to be defeated to some extent.*" It is when His will is *defeated* that we find ourselves in trouble.

It is difficult for us to understand the reason for pain and suffering. We do not understand why life has to be so hard. If we were in charge, things would be much better for everyone, or so we like to tell ourselves. I have been angry with God, I have argued with Him, and I do not understand the reason for many things that happen, but I have come to a place where I put my complete faith in the God of the Bible, in Jesus Christ, in the Holy Spirit.

It is a long, hard struggle, but we have been told from the very beginning that to reach God is to participate in a long, hard struggle. It is the reward at the end of the struggle that makes it all worthwhile. There is nothing more rewarding in the end than allowing God to lead you through this spiritual journey towards holiness.

The pain and suffering we encounter does not come from God as a punishment. He loves us and desires our happiness. Most of the suffering and pain comes from disobedience to the laws of God, but sometimes our faith is being tested, and sometimes pain and suffering are necessary for spiritual growth. No one leads a sinless life. Not one of us can expect a perfectly happy life, because not one of us is a perfect person. There is a perfect standard, but very few people care very much about striving for excellence or perfection in today's society. If we would teach our children to work to the best of their abilities and to follow the laws of God to the best of their abilities, we might be able to solve some of our problems.

The difference between right and wrong has become so blurred today. The truth of God has become so maligned that we no longer believe that we actually offend God. We must recognize sin as an offence to God. It should be obvious to anyone seeking the truth that we are straying further and further away from God and playing into the hands of Satan. We must ask ourselves how long God will let this go on.

Two sins that most of us commit everyday are ingratitude and a lack of humility. The sins of pride, arrogance, and selfishness make us think we are greater than we really are. Our real importance and greatness are only in the eyes of God, not in the eyes of our fellow men. It is how God perceives us that really matters, because He is the only one who really knows what is in our hearts and minds. We may be able to deceive our fellow men for a time, but we can never deceive God.

We may be laughing at the idea of God's will for our lives, and we seem to be living lives void of His will, but in the end, the will of God will prevail, and let us all hope that we will find forgiveness. We have the promise of forgiveness, if we come to Him in prayer and repentance. It is God's desire to bring each one of us to heaven.

A Better Day

May the God of hope fill you with all joy and peace as
you trust in Him, so that you may overflow with hope
by the power of the Holy Spirit.
Romans 15:13

There are some signs of hope. As I see more and more young men and women rejecting many of the liberal and modern views and practices, I see hope for our young people and their future. They have grown up in a society of relativism that has emphasized that there are no actual moral truths, that ethical and religious truths are a matter of individual interpretation. These young people feel that there is more to life than what they have been exposed to, and that they are experiencing a "spiritual hunger."

It seems as if God always works in forty-year periods, and I believe we may be coming out of our forty years in the wilderness. There is a great similarity between the Israelites and our modern society. The Israelites were not happy with the manna God sent them; there were many complaints against God. We, also, have been a very ungrateful society. We have more material things than any other generation has ever hoped for, and we do nothing but complain.

I wish I could understand why so many of the Christian clergy, both Protestant and Catholic, began to turn away from the teachings of their faith. I have to believe their intentions were good and that in their misguided sense of compassion, they felt that compassion took precedence over everything, even God's laws. However, misguided compassion can lead to a dependency state, unless all the problems are properly addressed. These liberal clergy seem to have forgotten that God does not condone sin. In order to relax or water down the moral teachings of traditional religion, it was necessary to remove the idea of sin. Once this was done, and God was relegated to a non-judgmental, tolerant, and benevolent benefactor, whose only interest in us is that we are happy, it was not difficult to slide down the slope of moral degeneration. For some reason, these men and women of God do not see that they have turned against God when they condone sin. They have forgotten their purpose. They were called by God not only to minister to the material needs of their flock, but, more importantly, to save souls, by preaching the gospel and by bringing those in their care to Jesus Christ. It is also very problematic to me that these liberal clergy who do not accept the Christian message feel that they have a right to create a new religion and continue to call it Christianity. I find it very difficult to understand how or why one who does not believe that Jesus Christ died for our sins, rose from the dead, and will come to judge the living and the dead would want to call himself or herself a Christian. Becoming a Christian is a choice - - a choice to become a follower of Jesus Christ. It would be better for all of us if those who wish to change traditional Christianity to a new Christianity would admit that they wish to create a new religion, so that so many would not have been deceived.

When we fall out of touch with God, it becomes more and more difficult to resist the temptations that come our way. It is a lot easier to do what is wrong than to do what is right. God asks two things of us. He asks for our faith, which comes to us through prayer, and for our obedience, which comes from discipline and also requires much prayer. We cannot always change the circumstances we find ourselves in, but God can change our hearts to better deal with the problems that come our way.

I began writing this book out of great concern for the future of our children and our country. Persistent irresponsible and unquestioned lies from the mainstream media, and the liberal doctrine preached in many mainstream churches, have brought great turmoil and confusion to our society. Many of those who were born during the baby boom years seem, for one reason or another, to accept the status quo. They have accepted the premise that everyone lies, that no one can be trusted, that sex is a free gift to be used in any way one wishes, and so on. The secular ethic proposes that if we do not judge anyone, and if we are tolerant of everyone and everything, we are good people. There is no mention of sin. Everyone will go to heaven, if there is such a place. No one will go to hell, because no such place exists.

There is one lesson, above all others, each person must learn: "God comes first, I come second." That is humility, the virtue that so many have abandoned and replaced with a false pride. When we convince ourselves we know more than God or that we do not need Him, we are missing the whole purpose for our existence.

We have lost sight of God's holiness. Because He is holy (perfect in every way) and because He created us in His image, we were also meant to be perfect. However, He chose to give us free will with which we could choose Him and holiness, or choose to rebel against His will; everyone of us, at one time or another, has chosen to rebel against His will. We have blinded ourselves to the truth of God. He never intended that we live our lives without Him. His desire is to have a personal relationship with each one of us. That is why God, the Father, sent Jesus Christ, who sent the Holy Spirit to help us with our daily struggles and to bring us to eternal salvation.

If we are to believe that liberal Christianity has replaced traditional Christianity, we would have to believe that God has changed His mind to accommodate our modern world. We have to believe that God is no longer interested in individual conduct regarding the laws He has set down, and that sin is no longer a problem. He has adjusted His thinking to our wishes, and now everyone will be welcome in heaven. Jesus died on the cross for nothing, since sin and redemption have nothing to do with salvation. Many Christians believe Jesus is their redeemer, but they also believe he was mistaken on a number of issues.

It is an interesting fact that the liberal churches are losing their members, while the more traditional churches are growing in membership. There is a difference between the real and the counterfeit, and hopefully more and more people, young and old, will find their ways to the true word of God.

Today, I am much more optimistic about the future of America and our children. I see young people who are seeking the truth. At one time or another, God calls every one of us. Some do not hear Him, and some do, but do not want to listen. I believe more young people are once again answering the call. These young people realize there must be more to life than sex and material possessions. They are trying to balance moral truth with the social issues of their time, as well as the tolerance and the acceptance of others. None of these issues can be abandoned. Jesus taught us to search for the proper balance.

These young people are trying to keep their faith in a world that they see going in the wrong direction. Rather than trying to impose their religious beliefs on others, they simply hope to bring God back into a society that has abandoned Him. This is a very hopeful sign. God gave you the gift of life. Be thankful. He is your Father, your Savior, and your inspiration to do good. Do not ignore Him.

Bibliography

Chalfant, John W. *America – A Call To Greatness, Winter Park: America – A Call To Greatness, Inc. 2003.*

Coral Ridge Ministries, *Reclaiming America for Christ Conference,* Fort Lauderdale: Coral Ridge Ministries 1997.

Carrroll, Colleen. *The New Faithful.* Chicago: Loyola Press, 2002.

Connell, Janice. *Mary, Queen of Angels.* New York: MJF Books, 1999.

Collinson, Diane. *Fifty Major Philosophers.* London: Croom Helm LTD, 1978.

Boyd, Gregory A., *Is God To Blame?, Downers Grove, Illinois, InterVarcity Press*

Federer, William J. *America's God and Country Encyclopedia of Quotations.* Coppell, TX: Fame Publishing, 1994.

Frost Jr., S.E. *Basic Teachings of the Great Philosophers.* Garden City: Doubleday, 1942.

Gibson, John. *The War on Christmas.* New York: Penguin Group, 2005.

Jorstad, Erling. *Being Religious in America.* Minneapolis: Augsburg Press, 1986.

Kennedy, James D. and Jim Nelson Black. *Character and Destiny.* Grand Rapids: Zondervan, 1994.

Kamenka, Eugene. *The Portable Karl Marx*. New York: Penguin, 1983.

Lewis, C.S. *Mere Christianity*. San Francisco: Harper Collins, 1952.

Lutzer, Erwin W. *Exploding the Myth*. Chicago: Moody Bible, 1986.

Lavine, T.Z. *From Socrates to Sartre*. New York: Bantam Books, 1984.

Mead, Lawrence M. *New Politics of Poverty*. New York: BasicBooks (Harper Collins), 1998.

Maddoux, Marlen. Free Speech or Propaganda. Nashville: Thomas Nelson, 1990.

Mannion, James. *The Everything Philosophy Book*. Avon: Adams Media, 2002.

McDowell, Josh and Bob Hostetler. *The New Tolerance*. Wheaton: Tyndale House, 1998.

Noebel, David A. *Battle for the Truth*. Eugene: Harvest House, 2001.

O'Connell, Hugh J. *Stewardship*. Liguori: Liguorian Books, 1969.

O'Connell, Hugh J. *Keeping Your Balance In The Modern World*. Liguori: Liguorian Books, 1968.

Oden, Thomas C. *The Rebirth of Orthodoxy*. San Francisco: Harper, 2003.

Schlessinger, Laura. *The Ten Commandments*. New York: Harper Collins, 1998.

Schmidt, Alvin I. *How Christianity Changed the World*. Grand Rapids: Zondervan, 2004.

Sears, Alan and Craig Astin. *The ACLU vs. America*. Nashville: Brodman & Holman, 2005.

Shiflett, Dave. *Exodus*. New York: Penguin Group, 2005.

Warren, Rick, *The Purpose Driven Life*, Grand Rapids: Zondervan, *2002.*

Whitehead, John W. *Politically Correct*. Chicago: Moody Press, 1995.

Whitehead, John W. *State vs. Parents*. Chicago: Moody Press, 1995.